# EASY-TO-MAKE
# LEARNING TOYS

## 50 Simple Wood Projects

• • • • •

# JOHN COXON

Sterling Publishing Co., Inc.   New York

Edited by Carol Palmer

**Library of Congress Cataloging-in-Publication Data**

Coxon, John.
  Easy-to-make learning toys.

  Includes index.
  1. Wooden toy making.   2. Educational toys.
I. Title.
TT174.5.W6C69   1987        745.592        87-15906
ISBN 0-8069-6548-7 (pbk.)

Copyright © 1987 by John Coxon
Published by Sterling Publishing Co., Inc.
Two Park Avenue, New York, N.Y. 10016
Distributed in Canada by Oak Tree Press Ltd.
c/o Canadian Manda Group, P.O. Box 920, Station U
Toronto, Ontario, Canada M8Z 5P9
Distributed in the United Kingdom by Blandford Press
Link House, West Street, Poole, Dorset BH15 ILL, England
Distributed in Australia by Capricorn Ltd.
P.O. Box 665, Lane Cove, NSW 2066
*Manufactured in the United States of America*

*For Daniel Wynford Richards*

## Special thanks to

Jackie Wells, who typed and corrected my manuscript so meticulously.

Bev Harrow, who photographed all the toys so carefully and sensitively.

English Abrasives in London, England, and Caroline Shears, for technical information about industrial abrasives and for their encouragement.

Colleagues at work and numerous good friends who offered advice and encouragement during the production of the book.

My children, Joe, Jack and Tom, who inspired me to make toys, tested them innocently and looked after them so well.

My wife Hilary, for her love and patience while I worked on the book.

My mother and father whom I love, and who still smile at what I try to do.

# Table of Contents

Color Section follows p.   *64*

# PREFACE

Most people appreciate the value of good quality, durable toys in the process of a young child's development. Toys that break easily and cannot be repaired suggest an insecure world where things are used and thrown away rather than cherished and enjoyed throughout childhood. Young children naturally appreciate and value toys made specially for them. If they are able to watch you at work, they not only get an object lesson in self-reliance, but also learn about the proper use of tools and the properties of materials.

My own enthusiasm for wood and tools stems from watching my father at work when I was a child. The independence and care he demonstrated, I inherited and hope to pass on to his grandchildren.

I began making wooden toys after our first child was born. The increasing pile of broken and discarded plastic toys beyond repair—the casualties of the playroom battlefield—encouraged me to start making my own. I saw many attractive wooden toys for sale, but they seemed very expensive for such simple constructions. (Nearly all the toys in this book were made from scraps and off-cuts of wood, and cost very little, apart from my time and patience.)

Apart from a few do-it-yourself jobs around the home, I rarely did any woodwork. My school days left me with a sense of failure (no doubt through being forced to make useless objects out of solid oak with impossible joints). It was not until I was 30 and a parent that I had my interest rekindled and my confidence fired by watching children at the school where I work making beautiful, useful and decorative things under the supervision of their woodwork teacher, Trevor Silson.

He gave me invaluable help and advice while I was making many of the toys for this book, and with his guidance I learned many of the tricks that enable anyone who is patient and careful to give a professional finish to their wooden toys.

The majority of the designs in this book are basic and simple, to give the beginner a chance to make nice things. There are also slightly harder projects to challenge the more able.

Woodworking terms are sometimes different in the United Kingdom and the United States. In this book, when they differ the American term is used, with the British term in parenthesis at its first mention.

I can't think of a more worthwhile pastime than helping to make young children happy. It is a two-way exchange —making homemade toys for the children, playing with them, and seeing them learn while they play makes me very happy. I hope you find the toys as satisfying (and relaxing!) to make as I did, and that your children enjoy playing with them as much as mine do.

# METRIC CONVERSION CHART

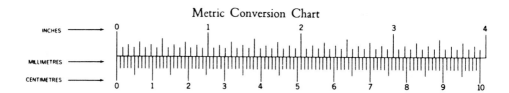

Metric Conversion Chart

# The Basics

## TOYS AND THE SAFETY OF YOUNG CHILDREN

Young children always seem to do the unexpected. Those toys we have lovingly made may be thrown, chewed and sucked, trodden on and fallen over. Parts will be pulled and pushed; so it is advisable to keep safety in mind.

Avoid using toxic undercoats and paints for decorating toys. Always check the label to ensure that paints are nontoxic. Round off sharp corners and edges when finishing the toys to reduce the risk of injury in the event of children falling on or throwing the toys.

Wherever possible, avoid using pins, screws and nails. Remember that even if these are concealed in construction they will inevitably appear if the toy is damaged accidentally. Remove damaged toys from circulation immediately and repair.

Supervise young children when they are playing with toys with small pieces that might be accidentally swallowed.

When choosing a toy for a child, keep their age and skills in mind. If a toy is too advanced for them to play with they will inevitably find another use for it that could result in injury.

If you let children watch you at work, always stress that they must never touch your tools unless you are present. I let my little children handle and use my woodworking tools under my supervision. I try to stress each tool's correct use and thereby imply that they should not be used for any other purpose, that each has a special job. They are responsible with tools because they are familiar with them and are clear about what each one should be used for.

Safely made toys last longer, as do the children who play with them!

## CHOOSING THE WOOD

The toys in this book are made from plywood or softwood (pine). Hardwoods are more expensive and far more difficult to work with.

**Softwood.** This is widely available from lumber dealers and is sold in stock sizes. It is usually planed all round and ready for use. When buying, state the finished dimensions you want, because, for example, stock 2″ (51 mm) × 2″ (51 mm) wood will in fact be a fraction thinner all round: you lose a fraction of the wood through planing. As a general rule, the "redder" the pine, the better the wood. Because wood is a natural material and is affected by temperature and moisture, the quality of the wood you buy can vary enormously. Look carefully at what you buy. Check for warping, excessive knotting and discoloration. Avoid damp or stained wood. Check for score marks left by the planing machine. Check for rough surfaces and splits. If you find a piece without these defects, *buy it:* you have already saved extra work.

**Plywood.** Plywood is made up of a series of sheets of thin wood called veneers. Cheaper plywoods have fewer layers of veneer, and often a thicker core with thin, often brittle, top and bottom layers. These thin surface layers have a tendency to splinter when you are cutting out, making it harder to get a good finish.

Birch plywood is stronger, has more layers and is less inclined to splinter when cut. It also has a clean, white and even-grained surface, making it easy to stain. In this book, wherever possible I have used birch plywood (the type used by toy manufacturers), but you may find it difficult to obtain. It is really worth trying to find. When you buy plywood, look at it carefully and avoid damp, marked or warped sheets.

## TRANSFERRING DESIGNS ON TO WOOD

Make sure that the surface of the wood is clean, free from grease and marks and is smooth. (Refer to *Getting a Good Finish*, page 14.)

To transfer my designs in cases where the drawing can be traced directly, use black carbon paper of the plastic type used for electric typewriters. The traditional heavy carbon paper tends to smudge and smear, and to be very stubborn if you want to erase a mistake on the wood.

Place the carbon face down on the wood, put the drawing over the carbon and go over the lines in a soft, sharp pencil. Plastic-sheet carbon paper leaves a thin dark line on the wood which can be used as a cutting guide. The lines can also be varnished over and used for guidelines for painting in details.

Some of the toy designs are too large to reproduce in this book full size. They have been reduced and printed on top of grids. To enlarge these drawings so you can use the sizes of materials given in the directions, buy 1″ (25 mm) grid paper or make your own. Draw a portion of the original pattern one square at a time. Make the line running through the 1″ square correspond directly to the line running through the book's smaller square. When you have the enlarged drawing, continue, using the directions given above.

## USING A FRETSAW

The fretsaw is necessary for making many of the toys in this book, and I am devoting a few lines to it in order to help anyone who is not familiar with using it.

The fretsaw is one of my favorite tools. It is relatively cheap and easy to master. It is ideal for cutting thin material into intricate shapes since the special blades are wire-thin. The blade is fitted across the springy steel frame and is secured by wing nuts (Illus. 1). Some models of fretsaw use ordinary nut-and-bolt fixing, but these have the disadvantage that you can't tighten the blade by hand.

Make sure when you fit the blade that the little teeth point downwards towards the handle. The cut is done on the downwards stroke. You may have to compress the frame a little as you fit the blade to give it tension, as a slack blade is harder to control and inclined to break quickly.

**Fretsaw Blades.** These are sold in bundles and come in various sizes. The thicker the material being cut, the thicker the blade. It is a good idea to buy a range of sizes and experiment. If, for example, you cut out a jigsaw puzzle with too fine a blade, the width of the cut may be so small that you find the pieces are locked together when you try to separate them after cutting.

Some purists suggest that you should clamp plywood to a table or bench when cutting out, but I find that I can easily hold the wood down with my free hand, which I also use to move the wood as I negotiate corners.

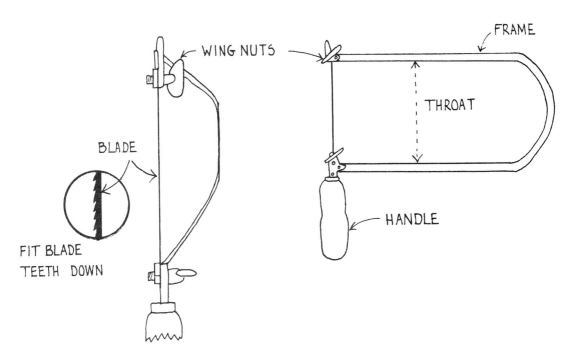

*Illus. 1. Using the fretsaw*

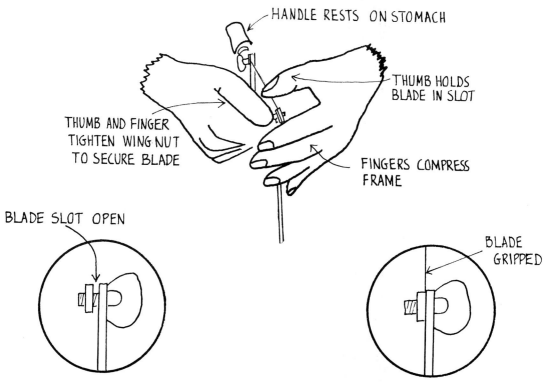

HANDLE RESTS ON STOMACH

THUMB HOLDS
BLADE IN SLOT

THUMB AND FINGER
TIGHTEN WING NUT
TO SECURE BLADE

FINGERS COMPRESS
FRAME

BLADE SLOT OPEN

BLADE
GRIPPED

*Illus. 2.   Loading the fretsaw*

**How to Load the Blade.** Check the direction of the teeth. Load into handle end of the frame first. Open blade slot by turning the wing nut. Place the end of the blade, teeth down, into the slot. Tighten the wing nut. Hold the frame between your legs with the handle pressed into your stomach. Open the top blade slot. Pull the top bar of the frame towards you and feed blade into the slot. Tighten while frame is compressed: it gives tension to the blade. You can use pliers to get the nuts extra tight. Refer to Illus. 2.

If you have never used a fretsaw before, load the blade into the saw and experiment with a piece of thin scrap plywood. Draw the outline of your hand on the wood and moving the saw up and down,

cut out the shape by cutting in from an outside edge, then following the outline with the blade.

Try and keep the blade upright and sit slightly sideways so that the frame doesn't catch your chest (Illus. 3). Avoid twisting or forcing the blade around corners—it will snap or distort. Make the blade "mark time" and turn the wood gently as you continue the cutting action on curves and corners. When you have cut out the shape, examine the edges. See the effect the blade has had on either side of the wood and check to see if your edges are vertical. Keeping the blade vertical in two planes is essential, especially in making jigsaw puzzles. You will also see how wide a gap the blade creates.

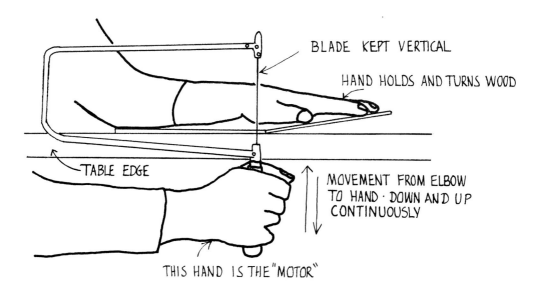

*Illus. 3.   How to hold the fretsaw*

**Internal Cutting.** Draw another hand shape on scrap plywood and pierce at the middle using a fine drill or by knocking in a thin brad (panel pin). Refer to Illus. 4. Load the blade at the handle end and

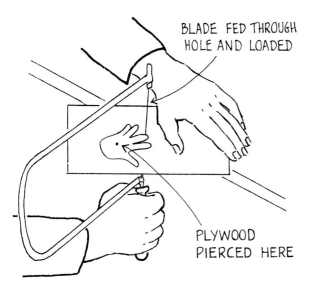

*Illus. 4.   Internal cutting using the fretsaw*

feed the free end of the blade through the hole from underneath the wood. Carefully secure the other end of the blade. Cut outward towards the circumference and trace the pencil line with the blade. When you have gone all the way round, release the topmost end of the blade. This technique is a little tricky, but it is needed to make many of the jigsaw puzzles described in the next chapter. You can practise loading the blade by using a piece of pierced sandpaper (glasspaper).

**Coping Saw.** This is a tool similar to the fretsaw, but it has a thicker blade and is used for thicker material. You can use a fretsaw to cut plywood and pine, but, obviously, it is harder work. (The elephant toy later described was cut out of ¾″ [20 mm] pine using a fretsaw. I should have used a coping saw!)

The thicker blade produces a rougher edge, and you should really hold thicker woods in a vise when using this tool. I use a coping saw with the same cutting action used for a fretsaw.

## END GRAIN

Most of the softwood we buy is planed all round; that is, it has been run through a planing machine, which reduces rough-sawn wood from the mills into a relatively smooth, regular material, so that the edges should need little effort to clean up. Only the ends, where the wood has been cut into stock lengths, are really rough, since any cut across the grain produces roughness. This is due to the "bundles of straw" cellular structure of wood.

"End grain" is the name given to fibre ends exposed by the saw cutting across the grain. When you cut softwood across the grain, the saw causes roughness which should be removed by sanding to give a more professional look to the toy. The end grain can be made as beautiful and smooth as the other surfaces. Coarse grade

*Illus. 5.   End grain before and after finishing*

sandpaper reduces this fibrous roughness, and then it is further reduced with medium-grade sandpaper. As a rule, if you can still see "dustiness" on the end grain, you still have a little rubbing to do. Finally, you can virtually polish the end grain with fine-grade sandpaper.

Illus. 5 attempts to illustrate how dramatically you can improve the look (and feel) of end grain, and reveal the beauty that the roughness conceals.

## CUTTING AND FINISHING PLYWOOD

Because of its structure, plywood has to be cut carefully. The problem is that the top and bottom veneers are so thin that you inevitably get some "fraying" at the sawn edge. To avoid this you can score across the grain of the surface veneer with a sharp utility (trimming) knife. This cleanly cuts the surface fibres, and when you cut on the waste side of your line any splinters fall away at the scored line, so that you get a sharp edge. This is particularly important when using "3 ply," which usually has an open-grained veneer that splinters and splits more readily than 5-ply birch-faced plywood.

If you sand the sharp edges of your saw cuts across the grain you may raise splinters; so rub over the edge in the direction of the grain.

## GETTING A GOOD FINISH

When a toy is assembled, it isn't really "finished." The most important step is yet to come, and it is the difference between a crude, amateurish product and a professional-looking article. Getting a good finish takes time, but the effort shows!

A good finish not only makes the toy attractive, it makes it safer and more hard wearing. Sharp corners bruise and injure the child who falls on the toy. Sharp edges are inclined to splinter and dent. So all edges should be rounded and neatened. The toy should feel comfortable to handle and smooth to the touch.

Two products hold the key to making a high-quality finish. They are *sandpaper* and *steel wool.*

**Sandpaper.** Wood is a fibrous material and sandpaper is designed to slice off the tiny fibres that stand out on the wood surface. The powdered and crushed particles act like thousands of tiny blades. The finest grades reduce these fibres to the absolute minimum, so that the wood feels perfectly smooth.

Quality sandpaper is worth seeking out; it has a longer life and is more effective. Cheaper sandpaper is "finished" by the wood; the wood takes off the particles rather than the particles taking off the wood! As a rule if the reverse of the paper does not bear a *grit number,* the paper is likely to be of inferior quality.

Sandpaper is sold in square sheets and graded according to the size and number of particles bonded to the surface of strong sheets of paper. On the reverse of the paper, usually next to the maker's name, you will find a grit number. The higher the number, the finer the paper. The lower the number, the coarser the particles. Thus 70 is coarse, 150 medium,

and 200 fine. Any paper coarser than a 70-grit number will probably leave more scratches than it erases.

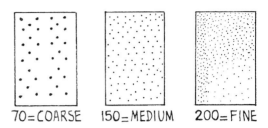

*Illus. 6.  Sandpaper grit numbers*

When rubbing down with sandpaper go from coarse grades through to fine (Illus. 6). Sandpaper is an abrasive, and coarse grades especially cause thousands of tiny scratches on the wood. You may not be able to see them but, if you don't go through the grades, when you varnish the scratches will magically appear and be highlighted by the varnish.

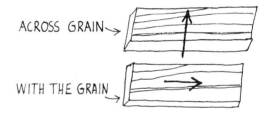

*Illus. 7.  Grain direction*

Rub the wood with the grain (Illus. 7). Rub across the grain and you'll put on more scratches than you have taken off!

Sandpaper can be expensive and the most economical way to use it for sanding by hand is to fold each sheet into four, grit to grit, and tear it into four sheets (Illus. 8). Fold it first, as tearing without folding wastes it! Then fold each sheet three ways, so that the gritted sides stop the paper

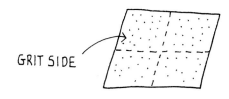

GRIT SIDE

*Illus. 8.   Fold sandpaper before tearing*

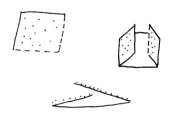

*Illus. 9.   Fold into thirds so sandpaper won't slip*

from slipping (Illus. 9). If only folded in two, the paper slips in your hand. You can wrap the paper over a small block of

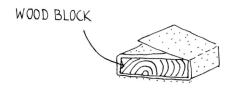

WOOD BLOCK

*Illus. 10.*

wood (Illus. 10). This speeds up the job, but the paper wears and tears quicker. Wrapping the sandpaper around a block of cork which has a bit of give increases the life of the paper.

The hardest part of the wood to get smooth is the end grain. If you leave it unsmoothed it is very hard to seal or paint, but with a little effort it can look beautifully smooth as well. Try wrapping a piece of coarse or medium sandpaper

around a flat file, and holding the paper on with your index finger, use the file to plane (Illus. 11). The hard file enables you to apply more pressure and eventually the end grain will look polished! This is the ideal method of rubbing down end grains and very rough edges.

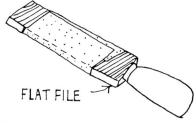

FLAT FILE

*Illus. 11.*

Your hands and fingers are the best judges of the quality of the finish achieved. Give it the touch test: if the wood feels smooth and comfortable, get the steel wool out, the sandpaper has done its job!

First, however, after the wood has been rubbed down, the wood and glass particles left on the surface should be removed by rubbing down with a lint-free cloth moistened with alcohol (white spirit). The dampness of these solvents raises the last tiny fibres left after the "onslaught," and when dry, this is when a last rub-down with steel wool is most effective.

**Steel Wool.** This product enables you to get the most amazingly smooth feel to softwood. It is sold in bundles in various grades and the thousands of strands of steel act like tiny blades to smooth away roughness. It also tends to highlight the grain pattern. It should be used to give a final rubdown to pine and also later to gently rub down the first coat of varnish.

# DECORATION

**Wood Dyes and Stains.** Wood, especially pine, has natural beauty and an infinite variety of grain patterns. By applying wood stain or dye, it is possible to color the wood, and still be able to see the natural patterns beneath. But children like brightly colored things. If you hunt around you will find that you can get any color of wood stain. You need not be restricted to shades of brown.

Stain is easy to apply, and quicker to dry than paint. Also, because the color penetrates into the wood, when the toy gets the inevitable rough treatment you can expect from young hands, marks and dents tend not to show.

Modern wood dyes are dissolved in alcohol or white spirit; older more traditional stains are water-based. (These may raise the grain of the wood and cause problems.)

Before applying stain, try a test piece first. It can be spread over larger areas using a lint-free cloth, but a small, soft artist's paintbrush should be used when coloring smaller areas and where more control of the spreading effect is needed. Where one color is to butt against another, I have found that the best way to prevent "crossover" spreading is to go over the dividing line with a sharp blade before putting on the stain. If the same brush is used for more than one color, clean it out thoroughly with the solvent recommended by the maker before starting the next color.

Stained toys need to be sealed with varnish. I use a fast-drying lacquer. Test on stained waste wood to make sure that the varnish used doesn't lift the stain a little. Avoid brushing varnish from one color to another if this happens.

**Painting on Wood.** Unlike stains and wood dyes, with paint you cannot conceal dents, holes and scratches in the wood surface by painting over them. Paint has the annoying property of drawing attention to minor defects in wood. So holes and other imperfections in the surface of the toy to be painted need to be filled with a suitable wood filler, allowed to dry, and then sanded over with fine sandpaper.

Before you paint wood it must be clean and free of dust and grease. After its final smoothing with fine sandpaper, take a lint-free cloth dampened with alcohol and rub gently over the wood surface. This removes grease, glass or wood particles which you may not be able to see. If this is not done, these particles will magically appear when the paint is dry!

Slow-drying undercoats seep into the grain of the wood, do not seal the surface particularly well, and may require several coats. With my toys, I use a fast-drying lacquer or varnish (known as precatalyzed varnish or lacquer). It dries in 15 minutes, seals the grain and is a good surface for most paints. When the undercoat you decide to use has dried, feel the surface. If it feels gritty, lightly sand with fine sandpaper and clean off before the final coat.

For a hard bright finish, I used Humbrol enamels which are widely available in small quantities. If alternative finishes are used, check that they are nontoxic. Check paints for compatibility with undercoats. Some paints blister on incompatible undercoats. I use good quality artist's paintbrushes for ease of control. (I don't enjoy constantly picking at stray hairs left by cheap, stiff brushes.) For fine black lines I sometimes use a cocktail stick dipped in the paint and stipple along the line with it.

Remember to stir paints thoroughly, so that the pigment mixes with the base. A second coat may be necessary to get a really nice finish.

## COUNTERSINKING SCREWS

Most wood screws have a flat slotted head with "tapered" shoulders (Illus. 12). If you just drill a pilot hole and screw them into the wood, the screw head will remain slightly above the wood surface (Illus. 13, top).

If you use a countersink drill bit, it will make a conical depression which will allow you to screw the wood screw down

slightly below the wood surface (Illus. 14). It makes the job neater, stronger and safer. If you want to conceal the screw, make the countersink hole a little deeper, and, having driven the screw down, simply fill the tiny depression with wood filler and smooth flat when dry.

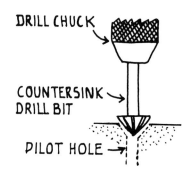

*Illus. 14.*

## CUTTING PLEXIGLAS (ACRYLIC PLASTIC)

To cut straight-edged shapes, score the line you want on top of the Plexiglas surface with a utility knife along a steel rule. Place this score line above a long piece of dowel so that the waste side of the Plexiglas is slightly raised. Hold the good side down to the surface and press down sharply on the waste side, and the Plexiglas should snap along the scored line (Illus. 15). It's like cutting glass! Do the same for the other edges that need to be cut. Rub down the cut edges with a small file.

To cut irregular shapes, cut along the line you want with a fretsaw. Be careful not to scratch the surface of the Plexiglas. File the cut edges.

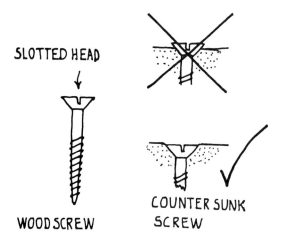

*Illus. 12.*          *Illus. 13.*

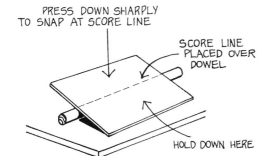

Illus. 15.   *Cutting Plexiglas*

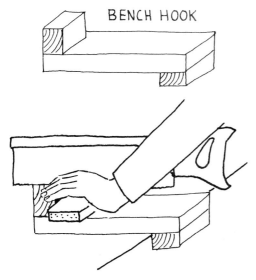

Illus. 16.   *Using a bench hook*

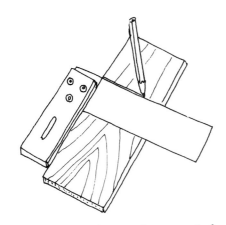

Illus. 17.   *Use a T-square (try-square) for marking*

## HANDY HINTS

1. If you have no woodwork vise, make or buy a bench hook, so that you can hold your wood on the table to saw. Lock the bench hook in your vise, if you have one, to make sawing easier (Illus. 16).

2. Use a T-square (try-square) to mark out your rectangular shapes and draw your lines lightly (Illus. 17).

3. When you are sure you have marked out accurately, score your line with a utility (trimming) knife to avoid splintering and to give you a sharp line to sand to (Illus. 18).

4. To prevent the underside of your wood from splitting when it is drilled, use a C-clamp (G cramp) and clamp the wood to a piece of waste wood. Place a thin piece of scrap plywood between

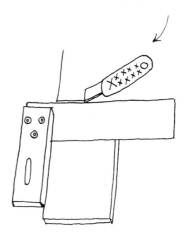

Illus. 18.   *Use a utility knife to score lines*

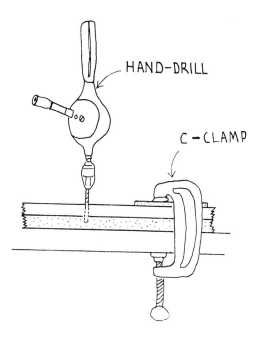

Illus. 19. *Use a clamp and waste wood to drill*

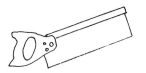

Illus. 20. *Backsaw (tenon saw)*

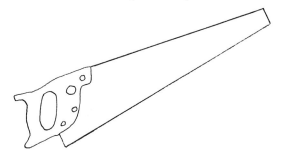

Illus. 21. *Handsaw*

Illus. 22. *Cut out on the waste side*

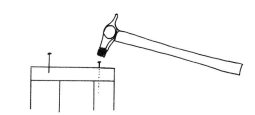

Illus. 23. *Pre-nailing*

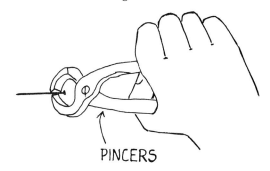

Illus. 24. *A home-made drill bit*

the clamp and your work to avoid denting the surface (Illus. 19).

5. Use a backsaw (tenon saw) for accurate and neat work (Illus. 20); larger handsaws (Illus. 21) leave a rougher edge and are less accurate; so they can make extra work.

6. Cut on the *waste* side of lines you have marked out (Illus. 22).

7. Hammer in nails shallowly before gluing. The wood then holds the nail and you have a free hand (Illus. 23).

8. Small drill bits often break; make your own! Snip off and discard the head of a 1″ (25 mm) brad with pincers. To make the drill bit, place the point of the brad in the drill chuck; the snipped end does the cutting (Illus. 24).

# PUZZLES

*I* have deliberately chosen to put tray puzzles and jigsaw puzzles right at the beginning of the book because they are the most straightforward toys to make, all children seem to love them, and you get immediate gratification because they take very little time to complete!

Apart from helping to develop skill in manipulating objects, puzzles help provide important early experience in matching shapes, colors and sizes, and in completing pictures. So play with these puzzles provides practice in vital prereading skills.

Very young children may need help to get used to manipulating puzzle pieces. They will learn more quickly if you show them and talk about what you are doing. Start by leaving them the last piece to put in. Then leave out another and gradually they will be able to complete the whole picture themselves. When they succeed give them lots of encouragement. They'll love it!

The great thing about wooden tray puzzles (see below) is that their popularity lasts. Even when the children have outgrown them developmentally they seem to enjoy the security of playing with "old favorites," particularly when they aren't well. Of course, they can be shared with younger brothers and sisters as well.

In the project drawings, solid lines indicate painting guidelines. The dashed lines show the suggested route for cutting the puzzles into sections. Often my cutting lines are chosen deliberately to isolate areas of the same color or stain to make decoration easier. Puzzles made with six to ten pieces should be suitable for most preschool children, but of course the same design can be cut into more sections to make the puzzle harder for slightly older children.

You will need a fretsaw and a supply of good-quality plywood. The best plywood, birch plywood, is sometimes difficult to get hold of, but it is the ideal material. It is strong and doesn't splinter when cut, and it is white so that you get a perfect background to offset any color you apply. But if you have to use the standard plywood most readily available in shops, try and get pieces that are as light in color as you can. Remember that when you varnish plywood, it tends to go darker; so wet your finger and dab it on the surface of the wood you choose to get an idea of how dark it will become. Remember also that the shop, if it has the facilities, will cut the wood to size for you, thus saving you sawing it into squares!

Inevitably the occasional piece gets lost. It's simple to make a replacement. Assemble the puzzle with the part missing, and place over it a sheet of thin white paper. Rub over the sheet with a wax crayon or soft pencil, and you'll get the exact outline of the missing piece to mark onto a scrap of plywood the same thickness.

# TRAY PUZZLES

Very young children can't usually manage traditional interlocking jigsaw puzzles because the pieces aren't held for them, and when they fit one piece, they soon get frustrated when the rest move. Tray puzzles solve the problem! They are constructed in such a way that an outline shape is glued to a backing piece which acts as a tray for the pieces.

The dog tray puzzle described next is a practice piece; it is simple and quick to make. I'll describe making it in detail, and then you can choose from the other designs which require the same techniques.

## Dog Tray Puzzle (Practice Piece)

**MATERIALS**

Plywood, ¼ " (6 mm) thick: 8¼ " (210 mm) × 5½ " (140 mm)
Hardboard: 8¼ " (210 mm) × 5½ " (140 mm)
Woodworking adhesive or P.V.A. (polyvinyl acetate) glue
Two pieces of scrap wood for use when gluing
Medium-grade sandpaper
Fine-grade sandpaper

*Illus. 25.   Dog Tray Puzzle*

Trace the dog outline and painting guides on to plain paper from Illus. 26. Cut out the plywood to size. Place carbon paper face down on the plywood; put your tracing over the carbon paper and line it up so that the drawing of the dog is central and has an even border all the way round. Tape the tracing and the carbon onto the plywood using masking tape, a strip of tape in each corner. Draw over all the lines with a soft blunt pencil. Remove the two bottom corner pieces of tape and lift the papers to ensure that you haven't missed a line! Remove the papers when you have a satisfactorily clear outline.

The next step is to cut out the basic outline of the animal. The easiest way is to take the fretsaw and begin to cut from the edge of the wood. Having reached the pencil outline, simply cut along the outline, removing the blade by the same route as it entered. This will, of course, leave a small line.

The neatest way is to begin cutting on the outline itself; so you will need to pierce the plywood with a drill, nail or compass point. Feed the blade through the wood and lock it into the fretsaw, as described on page 13.

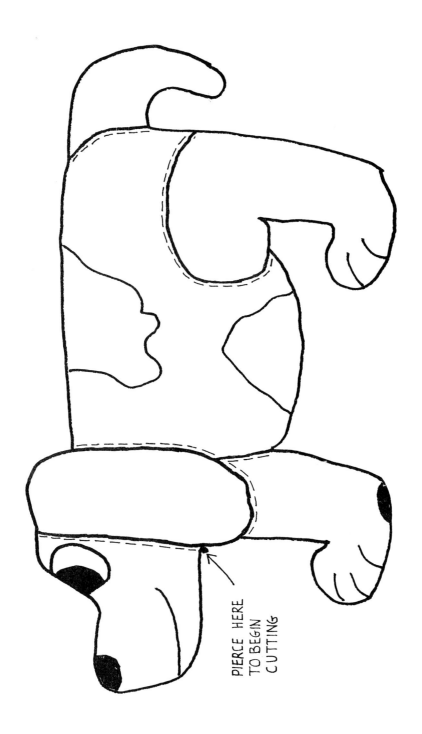

PIERCE HERE
TO BEGIN
CUTTING

*Illus. 26. Dog Tray Puzzle template*

Illus. 26 shows my cutting route. Remember, as you cut, not to force the blade or twist it. It may snap, buckle, or worse, give you a slanted edge which will make the pieces lock together; so try to keep the blade vertical!

Cutting should be effortless. The blade goes gently up and down continuously and you very gently push the plywood onto the blade, turning the saw as the line curves, or turning the wood with the "free" hand where necessary. When you get the knack it is so easy. (It's very frustrating having to explain something so simple in all those words; instead, I wish I could show you!)

When you have cut all round the outline, remove the blade and the outline shape. Replace the shape and see how it fits. Easily, I hope. Now use medium-grade sandpaper and rub down all the edges and neaten out any irregularities where you may have gone off course. Rub the edges of both the frame and the cut out piece on both sides (top and bottom).

Take off the sharp edges by rubbing diagonally outward on the top and bottom surfaces. Then rub gently along the flat edges. This method prevents splintering and also makes it easier to fit the pieces together.

You should now have the dog outline and the outline frame.

The next stage is to cut the dog into sections, following the dashed lines in Illus. 26. When you have your six pieces, rub down all the edges. Fit them into the outline and check that all fit.

Next glue the "frame" to the hardboard. Smear glue to the underside of the outline frame. (The shiny side of the hardboard forms the back of the completed jigsaw puzzle.) Put under pressure to dry, checking that excess glue is wiped away inside the frame. You could use two clamps and a couple of scraps of flat wood to keep the tray firmly under pressure while the glue sets. I used a few books and let the weight of the kitchen table do the job! Remove the glued tray when set and rub down the edges of the tray. Seal the outline tray surface. I used a thin soft-tip pen to ink over and enhance my design pencil lines and sealed the pieces with quick-drying varnish, having applied wood stain to color them. I'd already established on a scrap of plywood that the varnish didn't dissolve and smear the ink, but I dabbed on the varnish to avoid overbrushing just in case! (There is, of course, no reason why you shouldn't color the dog entirely with soft-tip pens if the color doesn't run in your experiment, but stains or paints will be most vivid.)

That's it. The following tray puzzles follow the same process. Color is added using either stain or paint.

*Illus. 27.*

# Hen, Rooster and Pig

These three miniature puzzles (shown in Illus. 27, 28, 29, 30, and Color Illus. C1) are the quickest to make. The dimensions of the rectangle of plywood you need to mark out and cut to make each one are as follows: Hen, 5″ (127 mm) × 4½″ (115 mm); Rooster, 5″ (127 mm) × 5½″ (140 mm); and Pig, 7″ (178 mm) × 4¼″ (110 mm). All three are decorated by using different colored wood stains, and they are deliberately cut into pieces which can be stained separately in one color.

Even before children are old enough to do these jigsaw puzzles themselves, they will enjoy helping you do them! Before children speak, they recognize simple words. Play "Get me the pig jigsaw puzzle" or "Show me the dog's head." It's fun and helps them to learn to talk. Let them try and put in the last piece! When they've gone on to harder ones, they seem to love going back to the old favorites.

*Illus. 28.  Hen Tray Puzzle template*

*Illus. 29.  Rooster Tray Puzzle template*

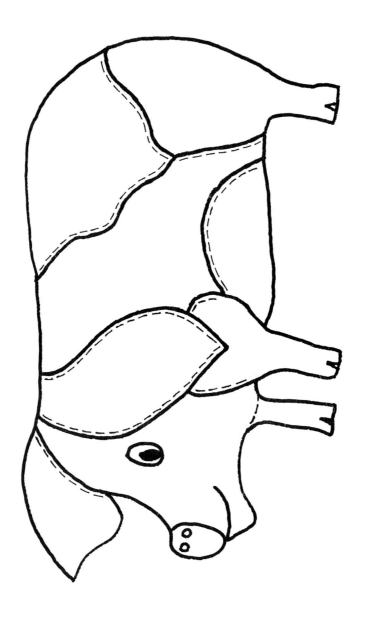

*Illus. 30. Pig Tray Puzzle template*

*Illus. 31.*

# Lion, Tiger 1 and Tiger 2

These three puzzles (Illus. 31, 32, 33, 34, and Color Illus. B1 and C2) combine both wood staining and painting for decoration. Apply the stains first and then seal the pieces with matt varnish and apply the paint when the varnish is dry. On the lion puzzle, the dark brown areas are sepa-rate pieces to make staining easier. The tigers' stripes are black gloss enamel. The dimensions of plywood needed for each: Lion, 7″ (178 mm) × 9″ (230 mm); Tiger 1, 7½″ (190 mm) × 12″ (305 mm); and Tiger 2, 12″ (305 mm) × 8½″ (215 mm).

Illus. 32.   Tiger 1 Tray Puzzle template

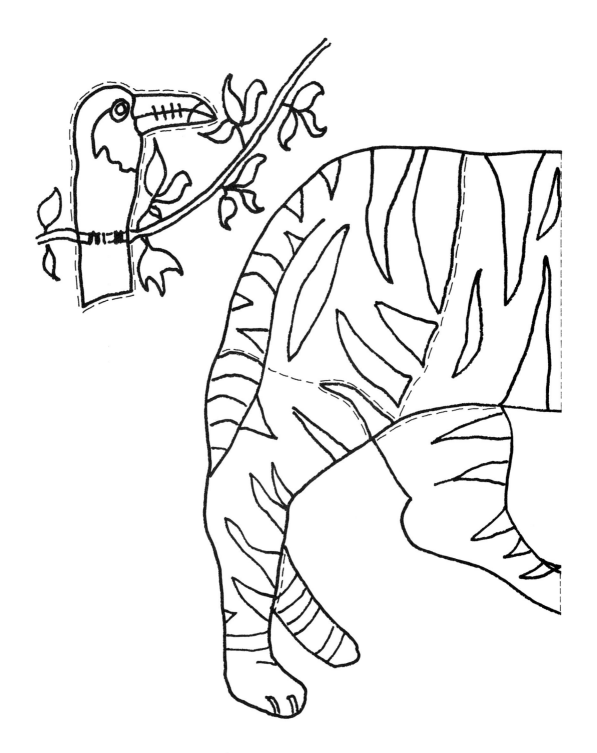

*Illus. 33.   Tiger 2 Tray Puzzle template*

*Illus. 33 (continued)*

*Illus. 34.   Lion Tray Puzzle template*

*Illus. 35.*

## Cats of Different Sizes

All the cats are different sizes (Illus. 35, 36, 37, and Color Illus. B1); so the toy is "self-correcting." The chests of each cat are left natural. Having cut out the five shapes from a piece of plywood 11½″ (292 mm) × 4″ (102 mm), dab the chest area with matt varnish and allow to dry before applying the stain.

*Illus. 36. Left half, Cats of Different Sizes Tray Puzzle template*

*Illus. 37.   Right half, Cats of Different Sizes
Tray Puzzle template*

*Illus. 38.*

## Number Line Tray Puzzle

To give a child the idea of the order of numbers, this puzzle is a long shape, 18¾″ (477 mm) × 3½″ (90 mm). Because the margin is narrow and the plywood thin (Illus. 38, 39 and Color Illus.

C1), use a softwood backing instead of hardboard.

Because of its length, you will have to cut out the border in stages from different directions, due to the restricted cutting length of a fretsaw.

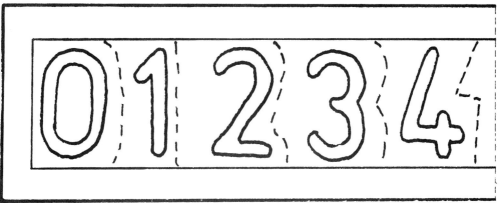

*Illus. 39.    Number Line Tray Puzzle template*

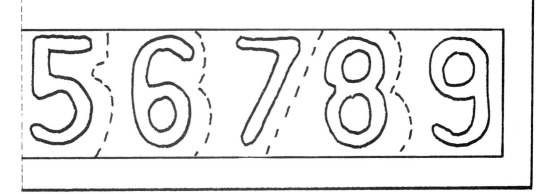

*Illus. 40.*

## Cat Tray Puzzle

The decoration of this cat combines stain and painting with white enamel (see Illus. 40, 41 and Color Illus. B1). The nose area was dabbed with varnish to resist the light brown stain which is applied to every other part of the outline. For the stripes, I used a soft artist's brush and applied a darker stain straight onto the cat. Experiment on a waste piece of the same plywood and see how the stain furs at the edges. Don't overload the brush or it spreads everywhere. Apply the gloss enamel on throat and paws after sealing the completed staining. The tray is 10″ (254 mm) × 8″ (204 mm).

*Illus. 42.*

## Duck Tray Puzzle

For this enamel-painted puzzle (Illus. 42, 43 and Color Illus. B1), use the same construction method as with the other tray puzzles. Instead of piercing the 10″ (254 mm) × 7″ (178 mm) plywood and feeding through the fretsaw blade, I cut towards the duck outline with my fretsaw from the plywood edge horizontally to connect with the waterline.

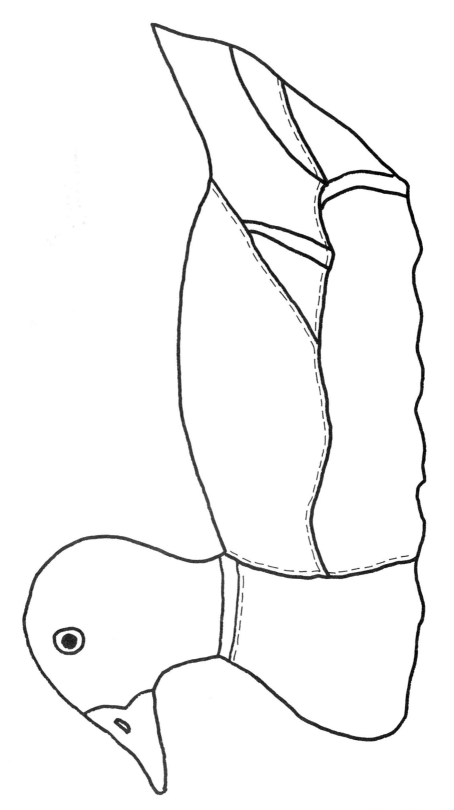

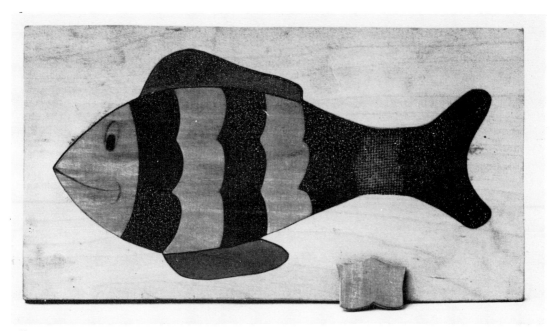

*Illus. 44.*

# Fish Tray Puzzle

This is another simple tray puzzle decorated with brightly colored stains (Illus. 44, 45, 46 and Color Illus. B1). The tray is 7″ (178 mm) × 12″ (305 mm). The fish is cut into sections which can be stained separately. Of course you can experiment with your own colors and designs. Why not look at some of the beautiful tropical fish for inspiration and make your own design and color combinations.

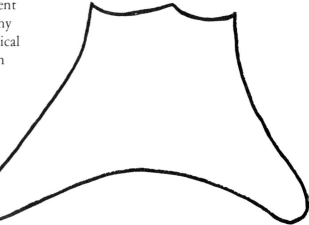

*Illus. 45. Tail template for Fish Tray Puzzle*

*Illus. 46. Fish Tray Puzzle template*

*Illus. 47.*

# Car Photo-Frame Tray Puzzle

Children of all ages seem to love personalized objects, and young children will be fascinated by a design which incorporates photos of them and other members of the family. This design is familiar to my children as our old car, and long after it has gone they will have this memento of it! Use this design to display your own photos. You can use a color slide of your own car as I did, or trace or "photocopy-enlarge" a suitable line drawing from your car owner's manual.

It is simplest to leave the window spaces empty, and glue your cut out photos on the tray base. In my example (Illus. 47, 48, 49 and Color Illus. C2), the window shapes are cut out and discarded, and replaced by carefully cut out pieces of Plexiglas that are the same thickness as the plywood (see *Cutting Plexiglas,* page 18).

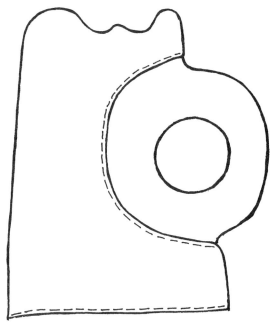

*Illus. 48.   Car Photo Frame template, right side*

The photos were glued on face up to the bottom of the Plexiglas. The construction method for this project is exactly the same as for the other tray puzzles already described. The plywood tray is 11″ (280 mm) × 6″ (153 mm).

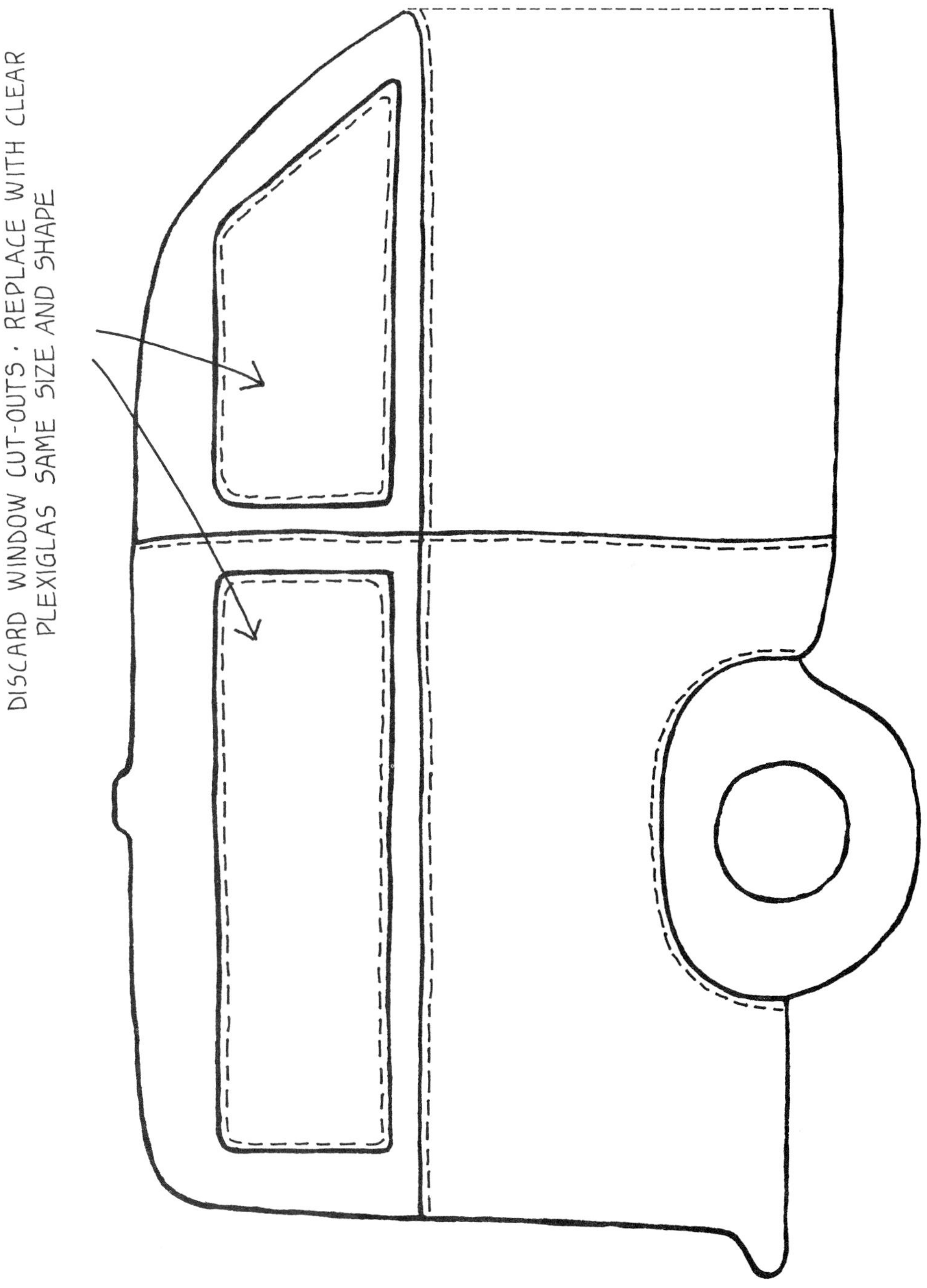

DISCARD WINDOW CUT-OUTS · REPLACE WITH CLEAR PLEXIGLAS SAME SIZE AND SHAPE

*Illus. 49. Car Photo Frame template, left side*

*Illus. 50.*

# Personal Name
# Tray Puzzle

Usually the first word a child ever writes is his or her own name; so why not make a customized jigsaw puzzle of it! Use the tray method described on page 23. Plywood that is ¼ " (6 mm) thick is the ideal material. The size of the wood you use naturally depends on the number of letters in the name.

Make the first letter a capital, and the rest lower case. The letters should be a minimum of ¼ " (6 mm) wide or they will soon be broken in play. See Illus. 50 and Color Illus. B1 for an example.

Use a thick marker pen with a chisel point. Draw the name in bold letters of a uniform height onto plain paper between

rule lines. When satisfied with the result, mark out your plywood to accommodate the name, and allow enough space around the name so that no letter is too close to the edge of the rectangle.

Tape a sheet of carbon paper face down onto the plywood with masking tape, and carefully position the name drawing over the rectangle. Tape it carefully in place over the carbon paper. With a soft pencil (not too sharp to avoid tearing the paper), draw over the inner and outer lines of each letter. Remove the carbon and drawing. You should have a neat outline for cutting out the letters. You should pierce the outline of each letter. When cutting with the fretsaw, you can compensate for irregularities in letter width. The internal cutouts in letters like "g" should be discarded.

# DOUBLE TRAY PUZZLE

*Illus. 51.*

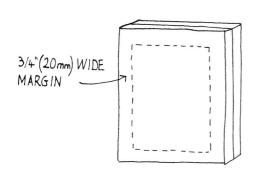

3/4" (20mm) WIDE MARGIN

*Illus. 52.*

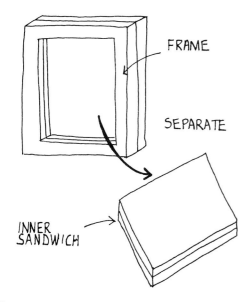

FRAME

SEPARATE

INNER SANDWICH

*Illus. 53.*

This is a lovely variation of the tray puzzle, in that two puzzles are sandwiched together. Remove the pieces of the top puzzle, and a second puzzle is revealed underneath (Illus. 51 and Color Illus. C2).

## MATERIALS

Plywood, ⅛ ″ (3 mm) thick: 10″ (250 mm) wide × 16″ (407 mm) long
Hardboard: 5″ (127 mm) × 8″ (203 mm)
Enamel paints: red, yellow, white, green, blue and black
Double-sided tape

Cut out two pieces of plywood 5″ (127 mm) × 8″ (203 mm). (I used ⅛ ″ [3 mm] birch plywood, but you could use slightly thicker plywood if you can't obtain the birch plywood.)

Use the double-sided tape to fix the two pieces of plywood temporarily together, face to face. On one face of the plywood draw in a margin border ¾ ″ (20 mm) wide (Illus. 52). Pierce one corner on the margin. Now pass a medium-thickness fretsaw blade through the hole and load into the fretsaw frame.

The secret to a successful double tray puzzle is in cutting out the margin. If you don't keep the fretsaw blade upright as you cut out the "frame," the pieces of the puzzle will lock in.

When you have cut out the inner sandwich, remove it from the frame (Illus. 53). Sand the edges smooth, check that the inner sandwich fits easily into its frame, and make any necessary adjustments by sanding with sandpaper.

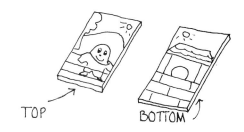

*Illus. 54.*

Separate the inner sandwich and mark each piece top and bottom, so that you know which puzzle to draw on each piece. You should now have two separate pieces of plywood. The next stage is to draw the two outline pictures onto the plywood by tracing out (Illus. 54). The top puzzle of the project given here is the "Humpty Dumpty" picture (Illus. 57). "The Cat in the Well" picture is copied onto the underpiece (Illus. 58). Remember to keep the two pieces of plywood the same way up as they were originally!

GLUE FRAMES TOGETHER

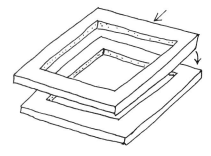

*Illus. 55.*

Having copied each picture onto its correct piece of plywood, the next step is to cut out each puzzle into smaller pieces. The cuts I used give manageable sizes and also isolate different areas of color, so that you don't have to wait for one area to dry before adding the next color.

Before painting, seal the illustrated side with varnish and allow to dry. Use a fine brush to apply the color.

The frame should now be separated. The two halves are glued together very carefully, so that they are fixed together in exactly the same position they were held in by the double-sided tape (Illus. 55). When dry, the hardboard base is glued to the bottom (Illus. 56).

HARDBOARD BASE GLUED IN PLACE

*Illus. 56.*

*Illus. 57.   Top of Double Tray Puzzle,*
*"Humpty Dumpty"*

*Illus. 58. Bottom of Double Tray Puzzle,*
*"The Cat in the Well"*

# JIGSAW PUZZLES

Children graduate to harder puzzles all too soon. When tray puzzles and even double tray puzzles have become too easy, they are ready for interlocking jigsaw puzzles. The tray puzzles can go to younger brothers and sisters.

When making jigsaw puzzles, there are two methods you can use to cut the interlocking shapes. One way is to draw the interlocking shape guideline on the surface in thin pencil. Cut out each piece and check that they can all be separated. Gently clean up the edges with fine sandpaper. Rub the surface clean of pencil marks and transfer the picture lines back onto the assembled puzzle. Decorate with stains or paints. Use a sharp blade on lines where you don't want the stain to cross over. This method is easiest: if you make cutting errors, you haven't spent ages decorating for nothing.

Alternatively, having cut out the outline, turn the outline over and draw the interlocking shapes on the underside of the work. Decorate the top side with stains and paints and leave to dry.

If you decorate first, and cut from the underside, the rougher cut will damage the decoration. (When the fretsaw blade cuts on the down stroke, the top surface has a sharp cut line, but you tend to get a rougher edge on the underside.) Simply put the fretsaw blade upside down in the saw and cut, underside up, along the shape guidelines. When finished you should have a sharp cut edge that needs no sanding. Just sand the edges of the undecorated side.

When you make your own designs for jigsaw puzzles, you will need at first to draw shape guidelines on the plywood. Examine shop-bought cardboard jigsaw puzzles and see how the interlocking shapes are formed. Divide your design into sketched squares of the same size and draw the interlocking shapes in, one for each side of the squares. Jigsaw puzzle trace-out templates are available from hobby shops.

# Parrot Jigsaw/Tray Puzzle

The parrot jigsaw puzzle is cut into tradi-tional interlocking shapes, but here I have retained the plywood outline from which the parrot was cut and backed it with hardboard to form a tray puzzle (Illus. 59 and Color Illus. C1). This is to aid youn-ger children who still need the pieces held in a frame while they connect one piece to another.

The plywood used for this and other in-terlocking jigsaw puzzles should be thin-ner than that used for inlay jigsaw puzzles. It takes less effort to cut, and is easier to cut with the fretsaw blade kept vertical when negotiating the curves of in-terlocking shapes. So you are less likely to end up (after all that cutting-out work) with a locked-together puzzle.

## MATERIALS
Plywood, ⅛ ″ (3 mm) thick: 10″ (254 mm) × 14″ (360 mm)
Hardboard, ¼ ″ (6 mm) thick: 10″ (254 mm) × 14″ (360 mm)

Prepare the plywood surface with medium and then fine sandpaper, and then transfer Illus. 60 onto the plywood. Pierce the ply-wood at one point on the bird outline, and carefully feed the fretsaw blade through the plywood. Cut out the bird outline. Sand the bird and frame edges smooth with fine sandpaper. Continue ac-cording to the general instructions. A template for the interlocking shapes is given in Illus. 61.

*Illus. 59.*

5/8" square = 1"

*Illus. 60.  Parrot Jigsaw/Tray Puzzle outline
and painting guide*

54 ▪ PARROT JIGSAW

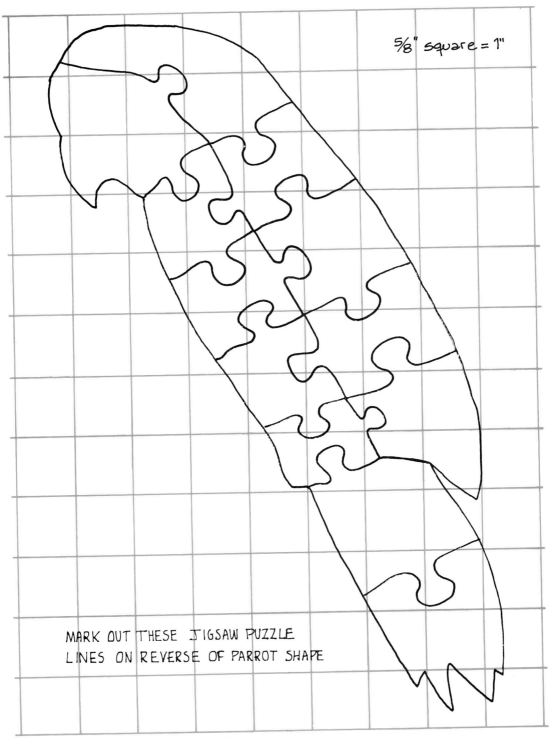

5/8" square = 1"

MARK OUT THESE JIGSAW PUZZLE
LINES ON REVERSE OF PARROT SHAPE

*Illus. 61. Interlocking shapes template for*
*Parrot Jigsaw/Tray Puzzle*

*Illus. 62.*

# Tortoise Jigsaw Puzzle

## MATERIALS
Plywood, ⅛″ (3 mm) thick: 7″ (180 mm) × 11″ (280 mm)

Draw the outline shape and features on 1″ (25 mm) grid paper and then onto clean, smooth plywood (Illus. 63). Go over the feature lines with a fine drawing pen (check that it doesn't run on waste wood). Cut out the outline shape using a fine-bladed fretsaw (the fine blade gives a clean cut and less sanding down is necessary). Smooth the edges with fine sandpaper.

The animal is decorated using dark wood stain. The light areas (see Illus. 62) are natural wood. Paint the places where you want to maintain the natural color with varnish. This seals the area and helps prevent the stain spreading from stained areas.

When the varnish is dry, apply the dark stain carefully with a small artist's paintbrush. Try to avoid overloading the brush and also avoid the "natural" areas you varnished. When finished, allow the stain to dry and seal the whole picture with varnish.

Turn the tortoise picture over and draw the interlock pattern (Illus. 64) on the reverse side. To avoid damage to the painting, you cut "upside down" along the interlock lines. Reverse the fine fretsaw blade in the saw, so that the neat cut is on the picture side. Keep the blade vertical throughout cutting. Sand each piece on all underside edges with fine sandpaper.

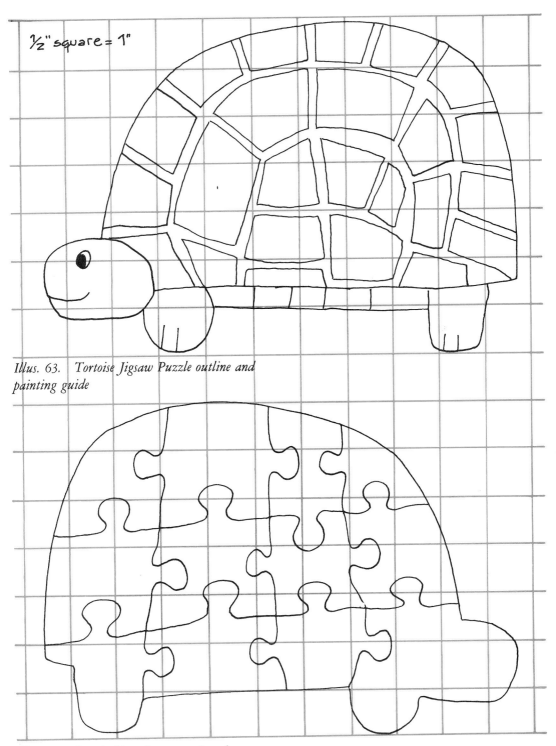

½" square = 1"

*Illus. 63.   Tortoise Jigsaw Puzzle outline and painting guide*

*Illus. 64.   Interlocking shapes template for Tortoise Jigsaw Puzzle*

# STACKING PUZZLES

*Illus. 65.   Ding Dong Bell Stacking Puzzle*

These puzzles act as freestanding stacking puzzles, rather like a miniature blocks set with a painted theme. These can be quite difficult for young children to do; so numbering each piece on the reverse side may help.

The secret of making these puzzles is careful measurement and marking out of the blocks. Draw marking-out lines using a T-square and a sharp, soft pencil. Mark the wood all the way round rather than just on one side; it helps you cut the lengths accurately. Before sawing go over each line with a utility knife to get neat, accurate edges. Remember to allow for the thickness of the saw blade.

# Ding Dong Bell Stacking Puzzle

This little puzzle is surprisingly difficult for young children but it makes an attractive decoration until the child is able to cope with it! It illustrates a nursery rhyme, "Ding Dong Bell, Pussy in the Well" (Illus. 65).

## MATERIALS

Pine (planed all round and free of knots and blemishes), ¾″ (20 mm) thick: 1¾″ (45 mm) × 40″ (1,020 mm)
1 Cup hook
You have to cut out 14 bricks (see Illus. 66). These are the various lengths you need:

## Wall

4 at 1⅝″ (40 mm) long

2 at 2¾″ (70 mm) long
2 at 2⅜″ (60 mm) long

## Cat

3 at 4″ (100 mm) long
1 at 5½″ (140 mm) long

## Roof

2 at 4¾″ (120 mm) long

When cutting with the backsaw don't rush or force the saw; let it do the work. When you are nearly through each piece slow down or the wood will splinter as the blade breaks through. Remember to slant the edge of the roof-tile bricks to give the pitched-roof look.

Sand each piece to take off sharp edges and smooth surfaces using first a medium-grit sandpaper, then fine. Take special care with the end grain and use a piece of sandpaper wrapped around a flat file to get a nice finish on the end grains. When each piece feels nice, rub over with steel wool.

Stain the wall bricks all over with bright red wood stain. Stain roof tiles with bright green wood stain. Seal with quick-drying varnish when the stain has dried. The middle cat bricks remain the color of natural wood, so that the cat stands out. Tape the three bricks together and trace the design onto the combined edges of the three bricks using carbon paper. The carbon line can be sealed with quick-drying varnish and this overall treatment of the three bricks (now separated) prepares the wood to receive the painted-

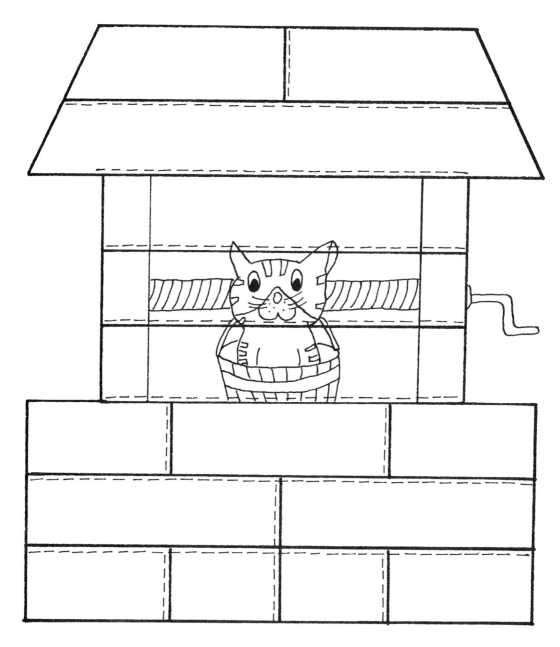

*Illus. 66. Cutting and painting guide for Ding Dong Bell Stacking Puzzle*

on details. The pillars are yellow. The cat is predominantly grey with a natural wood face. Bucket and rope are yellow. When main areas of color are dry, paint fine detail on with thin black lines. Lastly, screw the modified cup-hook "handle" into the edge of the middle brick as shown in the template drawing.

*Illus. 67.*

# Humpty Dumpty Stacking Puzzle

A favorite nursery-rhyme character with children, Humpty can be knocked down and put together again. The flowers on the wall help children to put the wall back together more easily (Illus. 67 and 68).

## MATERIALS
Scrap of knot-free pine, ¾″ (20 mm) thick: 5½″ (140 mm) wide × 7″ (178 mm) long

Clean the surface of the pine with fine sandpaper and steel wool. Use the template and carbon paper to trace the design directly onto the wood. Cut out the egg-shaped body section. Use a thick fretsaw blade or a coping saw. This wood is a little thick for a fretsaw and it's harder work; so a coping saw may be easier. Smooth all edges of the body. Using the backsaw cut out the ten brick shapes carefully. Sand and round off sharp edges with medium, then fine sandpaper. Rough saw-cuts can be reduced by rubbing rough edges on sandpaper placed on a flat surface. Stain each brick all over with bright red stain and seal with quick-drying varnish when dry. Paint the flowers and stems. Seal egg shape with varnish and paint. Humpty's face is the natural color of the wood. Paint on his facial features with a fine brush in black enamel.

Illus. 68. Cutting and painting guide for Humpty Dumpty Stacking Puzzle

# Designing Your Own Jigsaw Puzzles

Because they are quick and easy to make, jigsaw puzzles make ideal presents. I enjoy making jigsaw puzzles so much that I make some of my friends wooden jigsaw puzzles as "birthday cards," usually humorous ones with messages concealed under the pieces. The Cat Tray Puzzle on pages 38 and 39 was designed as a birthday card for my neighbor's wife who loves cats.

When you have tried some of my designs, why not have a go at designing your own? You can tailor-make jigsaw puzzles because you know your children's favorite characters, animals and objects, and you can choose the style of jigsaw puzzle and the number of pieces to suit the age and developmental level of your own children.

Very young "jigsaw kids" need puzzles of two or three pieces in chunky style (use ⅜" [9-mm]-thick plywood). Glue on pictures of familiar objects and cut in two pieces. The child can complete the object. Later, as they become more manually adept, use plywood of ¼" (6 mm) thickness. Interlocking jigsaw puzzles are best cut from ⅛" (3-mm)-thick birch plywood.

## COPYING PICTURES

Elaborate drawings are not necessary. Simple two-dimensional silhouettes of familiar objects and characters are most suitable. Don't forget favorite cartoon characters! Illustrated children's books are a valuable source of suitable pictures. You can trace and enlarge them, or even use an enlarging photocopying service. Also you can tape pictures to an outside window to create a "light table" and enable you to trace them.

## COLOR SLIDES

The Car Photo-Frame Tray Puzzle was taken from a color slide I took of our old car. I simply pinned a piece of paper to the wall and used the slide projector to throw the image onto the paper, moving the projector to get the image the size I wanted. Then I drew a simple outline around the projected picture. Why not try it with a slide of the family car or the house?

## USING PHOTOGRAPHS AND OTHER PICTURES

The easiest and quickest jigsaw puzzles are made by gluing pictures or photographs directly onto plywood. I used wallpaper paste—which reminds me that you could also use children's wallpaper! Use a rubber roller, if you have it, to smooth out lumps. You simply cut the plywood into shapes when the glue is dry. You can also use sticky-backed transfers which are commercially available. If you want to make traditional interlocking jigsaw puzzles, simply draw the interlocking pieces onto the back of the picture mounted on plywood. Be careful not to twist the blade or it will be a locked jigsaw puzzle!

# Birds and Animals

Birds and animals have special magic for young children. Some of the first words they learn are the names of animals; some of their first sounds copy the noises that animals make.

One of the delightful things about infants is their ability to play inventively, especially when they think that the grown-ups aren't watching. Soon after they learn to talk, they are at a stage in their development when inanimate objects are all thought to be alive, and have thoughts and feelings as they have. Originally I designed the animals and birds as decorations for the children's bedroom. Imagine my delight when I found that my young children played happily for ages talking to these toys as if they were real. I deliberately made families of animals, and these particularly remain firm favorites during private imaginative play sessions.

All the birds and animals in this section are made from scraps and off-cuts of pine, chosen for their bold grain patterns and for attractive knots. The graining gives a natural decoration and contour, and the knots form a natural eye on the design (Illus. 66).

So, look through your off-cuts from other projects and keep your eyes open at the lumber yard for wood with interesting graining and knots. All the birds and animals are made by drawing an outline shape onto the wood and cutting out thinner woods with a fretsaw and thicker woods with a coping saw.

The following designs are to get you started, but of course you can make your own designs. Use children's books with simple or silhouetted drawings of animals and enlarge them. All you need is a shape that is recognizable as a particular animal without any additional features. If the outline is right, the wooden animal will be right.

When you make these animals and birds, why not make templates out of thin plywood, for your child to enjoy drawing round as mine do?

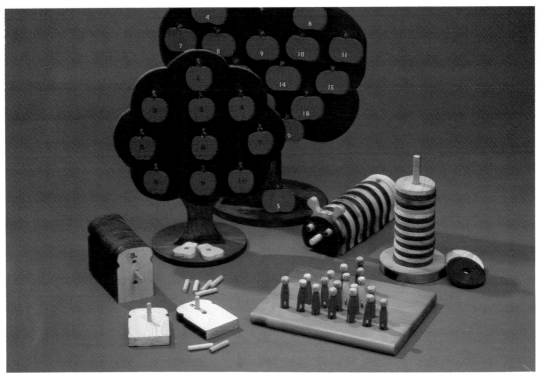

*Illus. A1.  Clockwise from top: large and small Counting Trees; Stacking Caterpillar; Stacking Tower; "Last Out" Pegboard Game; and Counting Loaf.*

*Illus. A2.  Decorative and useful toys, clockwise from center: Cat Pen Holder; Book Holder; Glasses Holder; Steamer Pencil Holder; and Old Boot Threading Toy.*

A

*Illus. B1. An assortment of tray puzzles. Clockwise from top right: Cat; Personal Name; Cats of Different Sizes; Duck; Fish; Lion; and Tiger II.*

B

*Illus. C1. Tray puzzles, clockwise from left: Parrot Jigsaw / Tray Puzzle; Number Line; Pig; Rooster; and Hen.*

*Illus. C2. Clockwise from top right: Tiger 1 Tray Puzzle; Double Tray Puzzle; Car Photo-Frame Tray Puzzle; and House Picture Frame.*

C

*Illus. D1.    Birds and Animals, left to right: Giraffe; Snail; Rabbits; Birds and Bird Display Tree; Squirrel; Mouse; and Elephant Family.*

*Illus. D2.    Action toys and games, clockwise from top left: Cat Fishing Game; Swinging Merry-Go-Round; Merry-Go-Round; Tractor; Plane; and Simple Racing Cars.*

D

*Illus. 69.*

Let's begin by making the birds since they are made from the thinner softwood, can be cut out with a fretsaw, and are very quick to make.

# Birds

### MATERIALS
Pine offcuts with bold grain pattern, ⅜″ (9 mm) thick: 4″ (102 mm) wide, with a small single knot in the wood of no more than ¼″ (6 mm) diameter
Dowel, 3/16″ (4 mm) diameter cut in 1½″ (38 mm) lengths

You will need pieces of wood wide enough and long enough to enable you to locate the eye circle on the tracing over the knots in the wood and also get the whole of the body outlines on the wood as well (Illus. 70). Copy any of the bird outlines from Illus. 71 on to tracing paper. Position the outline tracing over

the wood in such a way that the grain is horizontal and suggests feathers.

Having placed the tracing in the appropriate place, tape it upside down to the wood and draw over the lines with a blunt pencil. The pencil will make a faint line on the wood surface. Remove the tracing and go over the faint line to make it more visible as a cutting guideline.

Next, with a fretsaw with a fairly thick blade, cut out the bird shape. Sand all the surfaces with medium and then fine sandpaper. Round off the edges and smooth away any saw marks.

Usually knots in wood go through at a slight angle, and rarely does a bird or animal made in this way look right from both sides! So pay particular attention to the bird's best side and finish off by rubbing with the grain with fine sandpaper and then steel wool.

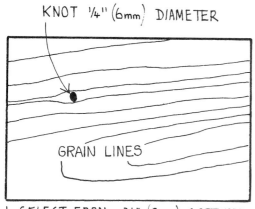

KNOT ¼" (6mm) DIAMETER

GRAIN LINES

1. SELECT FROM 3/8" (9mm) SOFTWOOD

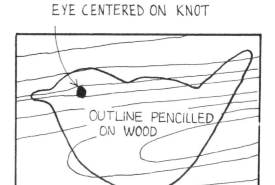

EYE CENTERED ON KNOT

OUTLINE PENCILLED ON WOOD

2. CENTER OUTLINE USING TRACING

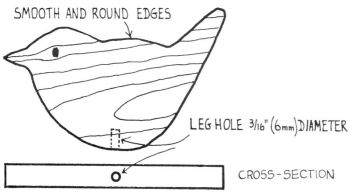

SMOOTH AND ROUND EDGES

LEG HOLE 3/16" (6mm) DIAMETER

CROSS-SECTION

3. CUT OUT SHAPE, DRILL LEG HOLE

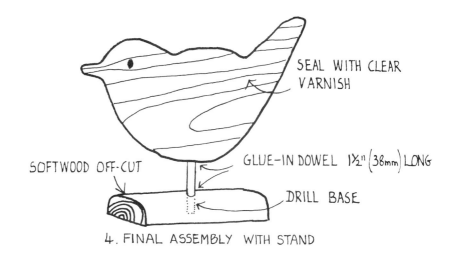

SEAL WITH CLEAR VARNISH

SOFTWOOD OFF-CUT

GLUE-IN DOWEL 1½" (38mm) LONG

DRILL BASE

4. FINAL ASSEMBLY WITH STAND

*Illus. 70.   Bird construction and assembly*

*Illus. 71.   Bird templates*

*Illus. 73.   Bird Display Tree*

A small hole is drilled centrally in the bottom edge of the bird's body to locate a short length of dowel which acts as its leg (Illus. 70). The dowel is glued into the hole.

At first when I made my birds, I had them "standing up" by making thin wooden blocks and drilling a hole in the blocks to take the thin dowel leg (Illus. 69 and 70).

Later I designed a tree display to keep them all together (Illus. 73 and Color Illus. D1) and mounted the "foot" end of the dowel leg into a larger diameter dowel to act as perches. I made the perches removable on the tree, because my youngest son loved to remove and replace the birds.

# Bird Display Tree

## MATERIALS

Plywood, ½″ (13 mm) thick: 7″ (180 mm) × 7″ (180 mm) to make the circular base

Plywood, ⅜″ (9 mm) thick: 12½″ (320 mm) × 15″ (380 mm) for the tree shape

Softwood, 8″ (200 mm) in length: 1½″ (40 mm) × 1½″ (40 mm) to make the trunk support

Dowel, ⅝″ (15 mm) in diameter: 6″ (152 mm) in length to make the perches

Countersunk slotted wood screw: 1¼″ (32 mm)

Lost-head brads: ½″ (13 mm)

You may draw a tree shape freehand on your ⅜″ (9 mm) plywood or use the pat-

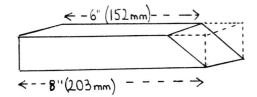

*Illus. 74. Trunk support*

tern for the tree shape given in Illus. 76. Trace the trunk template in the position shown in the small diagram.

## CUTTING THE PIECES

Use a fretsaw with a medium to thick blade to cut out the complete outline of the tree. Since the shape is quite large and the throat of the fretsaw is limited, you will have to cut the outline out in stages from several directions. Having cut out the shape, sand the edges smooth with medium-grade sandpaper.

Then, from the ½″ (13 mm) plywood, mark and cut out a circular disc 7″ (176 mm) in diameter, using either a fretsaw or coping saw. Sand the edges smooth to get a neat circle of wood.

Next, cut the trunk support out: mark out the 8″ (200 mm) softwood as shown in Illus. 74. Smooth the end grain and edges with medium-grade sandpaper.

## THE PERCHES

Before assembling the tree, four holes ⅝″ (15 mm) in diameter have to be drilled into the tree outline for the dowel perches. Arrange the birds on the tree and mark the positions for the perch holes to suit your arrangement. Place scrap wood underneath the tree outline and drill out the holes right through the plywood. Smooth off any splinters and roughness caused by the drill.

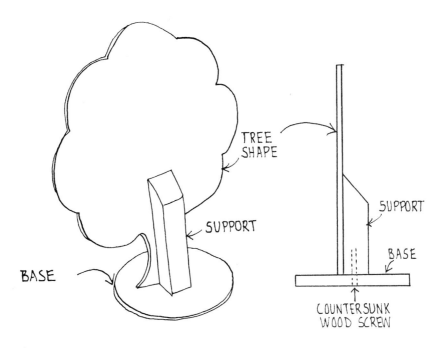

*Illus. 75. Assembling the tree*

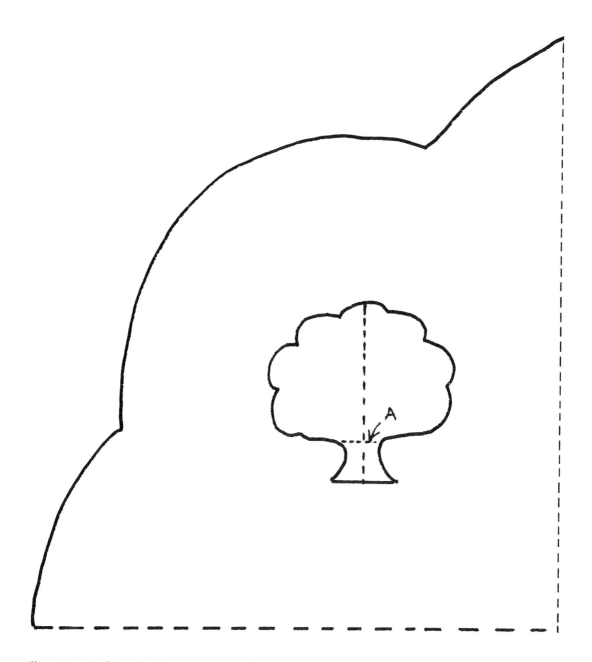

*Illus. 76.    Bird Display Tree templates and diagram*

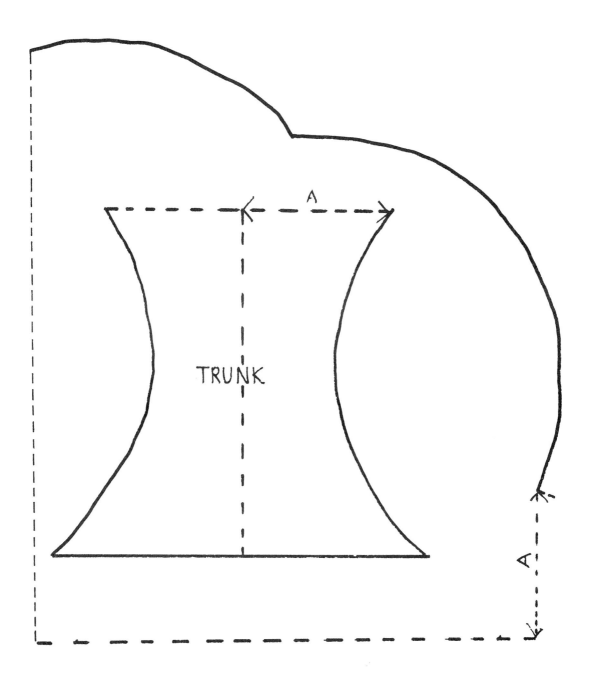

TRUNK

A

A

*Illus. 76 (continued)*

To give additional depth and strength to the perch holes, I made wooden blocks 1½″ (38 mm) × 1½″ (38 mm) and ½″ (13 mm) thick from plywood off-cuts and drilled each block centrally with the ⅝″ (15 mm) drill. These blocks I glued behind the perch holes on the tree, placing them carefully so that the drilled holes lined up.

For the perches, cut the ⅝″ (15 mm) diameter dowel rod into 1½″ (38 mm) lengths, taking care not to split the dowel as the backsaw is finishing its cut. Carefully drill a 3/16″ (4 mm) diameter hole ½″ (13 mm) from one end of the dowel ¼″ (6 mm) deep, vertically into the dowel. This serves as the hole for the bird's leg.

I glued the birds' legs to the perches, but left the perches unglued, so that the children could remove and rearrange the birds.

## ASSEMBLING THE TREE
To assemble the tree (Illus. 75), first drill through the center point of the circular base ¼″ (6 mm) and then countersink the hole on the underside. Place the trunk support centrally over the hole and push the screw through the base and into the bottom of the support to mark the position for a smaller pilot hole to make screwing easier. Spread glue on the end of the support and screw the base into the support. Wipe away excess glue.

Next, smear the facing surface of the trunk support with glue, and put to one side. Tap two or three ½″ (13 mm) lost-head brads into the trunk of the tree shape on the facing side. Position the tree evenly against the trunk support so that it rests squarely on the circular base. Lay the tree (face up) on the edge of a bench or flat table. Tap in the brads, making sure that the tree base is flush with the circular base. (Wipe off any excess glue carefully with a damp cloth, because stain will not take to wood accidentally "sealed" by dried excess glue.)

The tree trunk is stained dark brown, and the front and back of the tree is stained green. The circular base is also stained green. The last job is to seal the tree with varnish.

## VARIATIONS
As an extension of this design, especially if you enjoy using interesting pieces of wood to make different birds, why not make a much larger tree outline from plywood, decorate it in the same way, but have it hanging from the wall?
Attach the birds using screwed eyes and hooks. Or, draw and cut out shapes of birds in a nesting position and glue short strips of wood to the tree outline as nests for the birds to rest on.

*Illus. 77.*

# Rabbit Family

My children love playing with this rabbit family, and it makes a delightful decoration for their room when play is over (Illus. 77 and Color Illus. D1). I gave the rabbits names and invented stories which I act out for my children, moving the figures around their display. The stories are usually about baby rabbits lost and found or getting into mischief. It's nice to see the stories enacted by the children later, and very interesting to see what they get members of the "family" to do and say in their free play.

## MATERIALS

Off-cuts of softwood, ¾ ″ (20 mm) thick: 4″ (102 mm) wide

All three rabbits are made from ¾ ″ (20-mm)-thick pine off-cuts. The rabbits squat flat and the grain pattern is horizontal to the ground line. I chose wood with a

small single knot about ¼ ″ (6 mm) in diameter. (As you get more practice, you can envision the rabbit outline on a piece of wood and judge what will make an attractive and realistic animal.)

The rabbits are marked out in the same way as the birds and other animals, and cut out using a coping saw. Trace out one item at a time from Illus. 78. To make the second adult rabbit, simply reverse the large rabbit tracing and select an appropriate piece of wood.

With the rabbits, I spent more time and care rounding off the edges, first paring carefully with a utility knife, and then smoothing with sandpaper, going through the grades from coarse to fine to get a rounded effect for their backs.

Although this is sufficient to make an attractive animal, you can further enhance the toy by emphasizing the strong curve

Illus. 78.   Rabbit Family and Rabbit Display Stand templates

of the animal's back leg. I used a small woodcarving gouge, and cutting carefully with the grain, lowered the profile of the wood on the rabbit's body to make the hind leg stand in relief. Then, using medium-grade sandpaper, hand-held, I rubbed with the grain to smooth away the cuts and round off the feature nicely.

If you have never used a woodcarving chisel before, remember the golden rule: always cut away from you. Hold the wood with your free hand spread behind where you are cutting, and with the chisel in your working hand, cut away from you, clear of your free hand.

# Rabbit Display Stand

When the rabbit family is not in use, the rabbits are displayed on a simple little stand. The "hedge" shape is cut out of ¼″ (6 mm) plywood and stained green. The hedge outline is made large enough so that from most angles, the pale rabbits have a dark green background to make them stand out in a room.

## MATERIALS
Plywood, ¼″ (6 mm) thick: 8″ (203 mm) × 5½″ (140 mm)

Softwood, ¾″ (20 mm) thick: 6½″ (165 mm) × 4½″ (110 mm)

Trace the hedge shape (Illus. 78) on to a piece of plywood 5½″ (140 mm) × 8″ (203 mm) and cut out the shape with a medium-blade fretsaw. Sand and smooth the edges with medium, then fine sandpaper, taking care to erase any potential splinters! Smooth the front surface and wipe clean. Apply green wood stain to all the edges and front and rear surfaces.

Next cut out a rectangle of softwood ¾″ (20 mm) thick and 6½″ (165 mm) long × 4½″ (110 mm) wide. Use sandpaper to smooth the edges. Then, screw or nail and glue the hedge to the base (Illus. 79), and wipe away excess glue with a damp cloth. Seal with varnish.

For my stand, to make the base block a little more like a small mound, I planed the front and side edges of the base and rounded them off with sandpaper. The revealed grain gave a contoured look.

The base should also be stained green, but will be much paler, since the softwood absorbs less stain than the porous plywood back. Don't forget to seal the base with varnish.

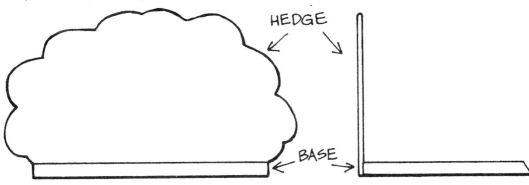

*Illus. 79. Display Stand assembly*

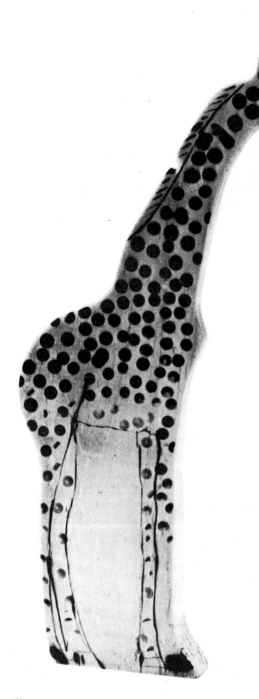

*Illus. 80.*

## Giraffe

### MATERIALS
Softwood, ¾″ (20 mm) thick: 10½″ (268 mm) × 5½″ (140 mm)

The giraffe is made from a featureless, knot-free piece of softwood which has no vivid grain pattern (see above and Color Illus. D1). The shape and features are traced and transferred onto the wood.

Having cut out the basic shape (Illus. 81) with a coping saw (I used a fretsaw to cut out the ears and "horn") smooth saw scars out on the cut edges, and get the edges smooth. Do not cut the spaces between the legs. On this animal, round off the edges only enough to get rid of the sharpness.

To suggest the pattern of the giraffe's hide, I burned on spots. Cut the head off a 4″ (100 mm) nail with a hacksaw and holding the cut end of the nail in a pair of pliers, heat the nailhead over a stove (gas ring); then carefully stamp on the pattern using the nailhead. The lines on the animal were drawn with a heated needle.

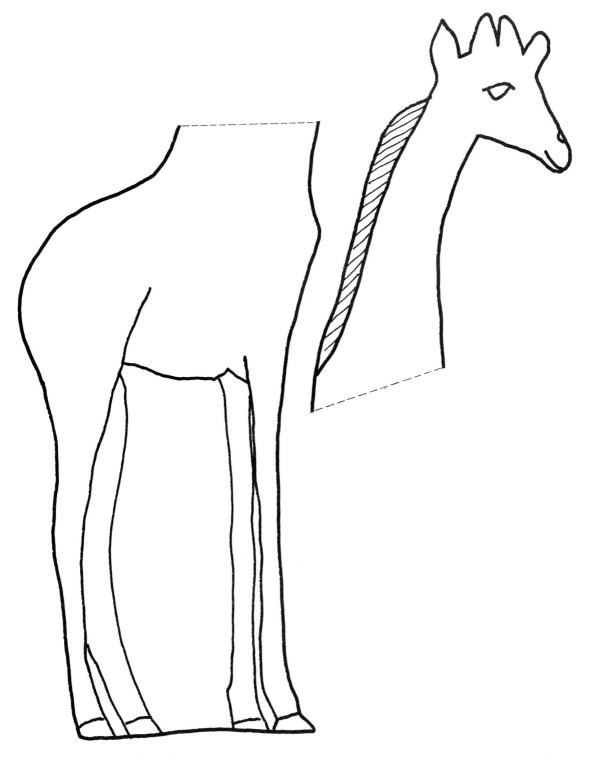

*Illus. 81.   Giraffe template*

*Illus. 82.*

# Elephant Family

## MATERIALS

Pine, 2 pieces, each ¾ " (20 mm) thick: 6½ " (165 mm) × 4½ " (115 mm)
Pine, ¾ " (20 mm) thick: 3¼ " (83 mm) × 4½ " (115 mm)
Thin scrap softwood for ears (optional)

Try and select lumber with similar grain pattern and knotting for each of the family. Cut out with a coping saw. Sand and round off edges on both sides of the wood, but avoid rounding the edges too much or the animal will lose its "chunky" look. (I used large knots for the eyes as a personal preference, as above and in Color Illus. D1. You may prefer to use much smaller knots for eyes, as real elephants have relatively tiny eyes!)

In Illus. 83 and 84 I have shown the ear lines, since you may wish to cut out ear shapes from thinner softwood and glue them in place to add interest.

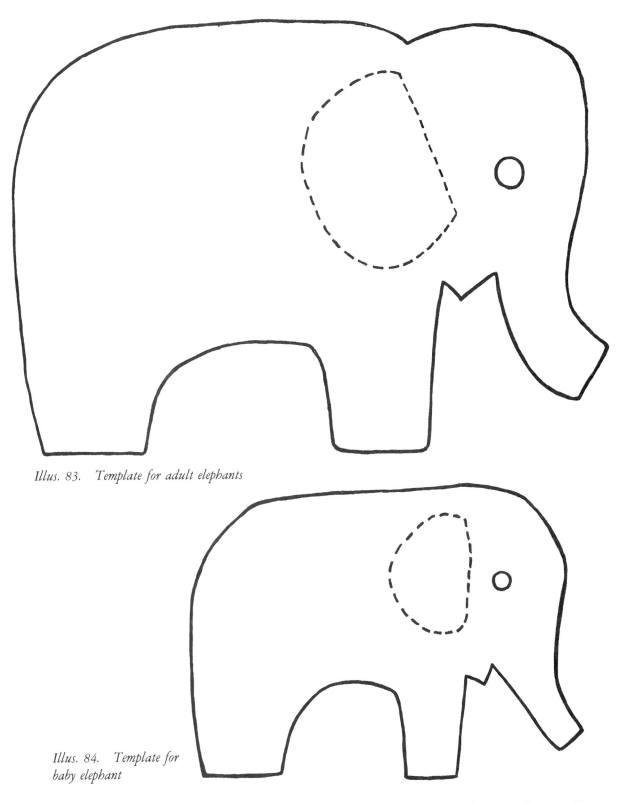

*Illus. 83.* *Template for adult elephants*

*Illus. 84. Template for baby elephant*

*Illus. 85.*

# Mouse

Cut from an off-cut of ½″ (13 mm) soft-wood with a stripy grain and a nice circular, dark knot of ⅛″ (3 mm) diameter. Use a fretsaw with medium blade to cut out. The nose is slightly tapered; the edges rounded and smoothed (above and Color Illus. D1). Glue and insert a 4″ (100 mm) length of nylon cord ⅛″ (3 mm) in diameter into a hole drilled in the back edge (Illus. 86). Heat the other end of the nylon cord with a lighted match and twirl into a point using your thumb and forefinger.

# Squirrel

Cut from an off-cut of ¾″ (20-mm)-thick softwood. Follow the grain direction suggested in Illus. 87 to add strength. Use a dark, round knot for the eye. The animal here has been enhanced by narrowing the thickness of the body with a small wood-carving gouge, to make the head and hind legs stand out (above and Color Illus. D1).

# Snail

### MATERIALS
Pine, ¾″ (20 mm) thick: 7″ (175 mm) × 1″ (25 mm) for the body
Pine, ¾″ (20 mm) thick: 3″ (76 mm) × 3½″ (89 mm) with a central knot for the shell
Dowel, ⅛″ (3 mm) in diameter
2 wooden beads

The shell is a separate piece, screwed or glued onto the body (above and Color Illus D1). For the shell you need a smooth large knot in the wood about 1½″ (38 mm) in diameter. The body piece, 7″ (180 mm) long × 1″ (25 mm) wide, is enhanced with feelers and antlers made from ⅛″ (3-mm) -diameter dowel crowned with two small wooden beads (Illus. 88).

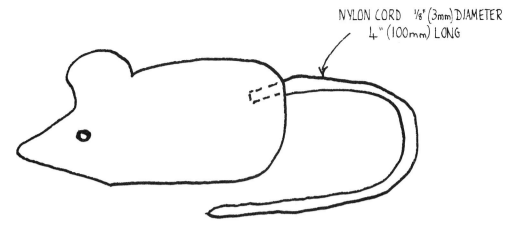

NYLON CORD   ⅛" (3mm) DIAMETER
4" (100mm) LONG

*Illus. 86.   Mouse template*

*Illus. 87.   Squirrel template*

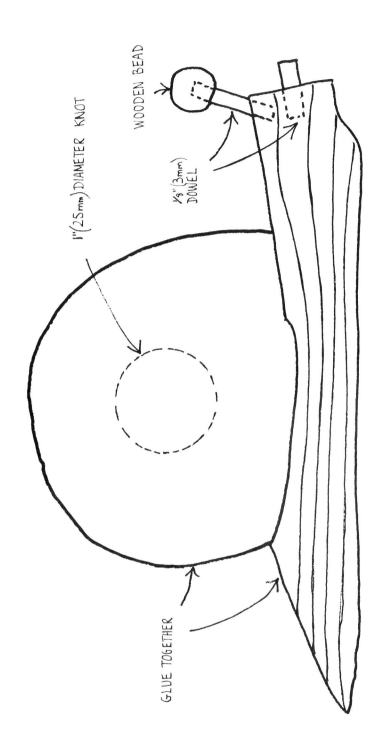

1"(25mm) DIAMETER KNOT

WOODEN BEAD

1/8"(3mm) DOWEL

GLUE TOGETHER

*Illus. 88. Snail template*

# Decorative and

# Useful Toys

## Glasses Holder

Children who wear glasses often lose or break them. This simple idea gives them a special place to keep them safe.

**MATERIALS**
Plywood, ⅛″ (3 mm) thick: 5½″ (135 mm) × 7″ (180 mm)
Quadrant moulding, ¾″ (20 mm) diameter: 11½″ (290 mm) long
Finishing (veneer) nails: 1″ (25 mm)

Trace the design (Illus. 88) on to the cleaned, smoothed plywood surface, and using a fine blade, cut out the outline with a fretsaw. Sand the edges carefully with fine sandpaper.

Next, carefully cut two lengths of ¾″ radius (20 mm) quadrant moulding, each 5¾″ (145 mm) long. The two strips of moulding are glued on either side of the base to enable the "face" to stand up (Illus. 89).

Finishing nails are used to hold the strips in place while the glue sets. (Finishing

*Illus. 89.*

*Illus. 90.   Glasses Holder template*

nails are fine nails which do not split narrow strips of wood, as brads would.) Tap the nails shallowly in place first before applying the glue. This leaves a hand free to hold the strip in position while you hammer the nails down. Wipe off excess glue with a damp cloth.

Varnish the front surface to seal the wood. When the varnish is dry, paint over the facial features and hair using black enamel paint applied with a fine brush (Color Illus. A2).

The child simply folds the stems of the glasses behind the "ears"; the plywood is thin to allow the stems to fold flat and the glasses to stay in position. (You may have to adjust the drawing to accommodate nonstandard frames. Measure the gap between the closed stems at the hinges and change the drawing if necessary.)

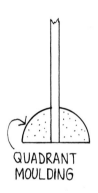

QUADRANT
MOULDING

*Illus. 91.   Diagram for base of Glasses Holder*

*Illus. 92.*

# Book Holder

This is a simple idea to enable children to keep their favorite books together. It is a simple "bracket" made from three pieces of plywood (Illus. 93).

## MATERIALS
Plywood, ½″ (10 mm) thick: 7″ (178 mm) × 10¾″ (273 mm) for the face

Plywood, ½″ (10 mm) thick: 7″ (178 mm) × 4″ (102 mm) for the base
Plywood, ½″ (10 mm) thick: 7″ (178 mm) × 7″ (178 mm) for the back
Brads (panel pins): 1″ (25 mm)

Copy the face design (Illus. 94) on to the plywood and cut out the outline shape using a thick-bladed fretsaw. Cut out the mouth by piercing the mouth line with a small drill and feeding the fretsaw blade through the hole and tightening the blade into the saw frame, then cutting. Sand all the edges smooth with medium and fine sandpaper.

Cut the base piece out using a backsaw. Try to get the edges as square as possible when cutting. Cut out the back piece.

Smear the 7″ (178-mm)-long edges of the base piece with glue and put to one side. Next tap two or three 1″ (25 mm) brads partly into the bottom edge of the face piece, so that they are held in place by the plywood. You can draw a light guideline parallel to the bottom edge of the face piece, ¼″ (6 mm) up, so that when you nail the face to the base, the brads penetrate centrally and don't split the surface.

If you have a vise, clamp the preglued base in the vise, position the face piece on the glued base edge, and tap the brads home with a hammer. Repeat the process with the back piece. Wipe off excess glue with a damp cloth.

Seal with varnish when the glue is dry, or use an appropriate undercoat. I used a dark brown wood stain for the hair, painted the facial features in black enamel gloss and gave the "man" a yellow shirt and green tie (Color Illus. A2).

You can of course use this simple method and designs of your own. I used the elephant outline (page 79) and adjusted the width of the base to suit, to make a holder for smaller books. By extending the length of the base piece, you can accommodate more books.

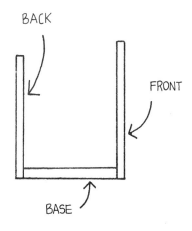

*Illus. 93.   Book Holder assembly*

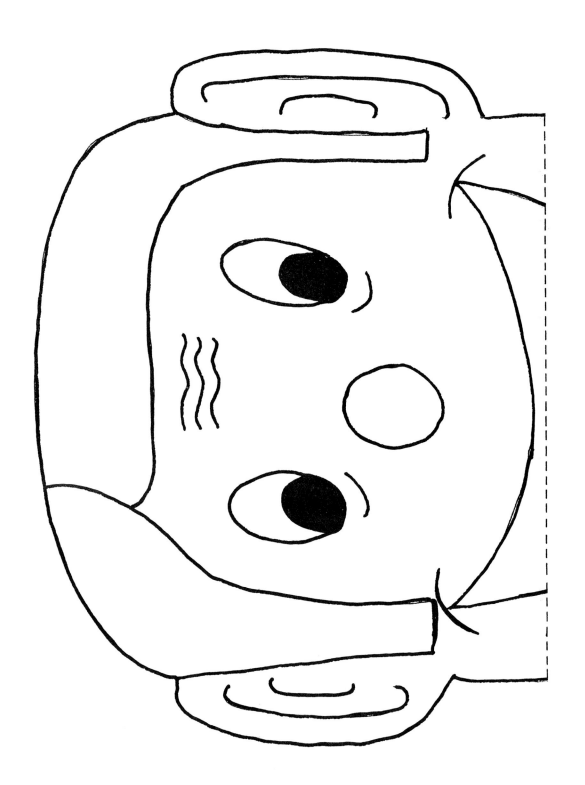

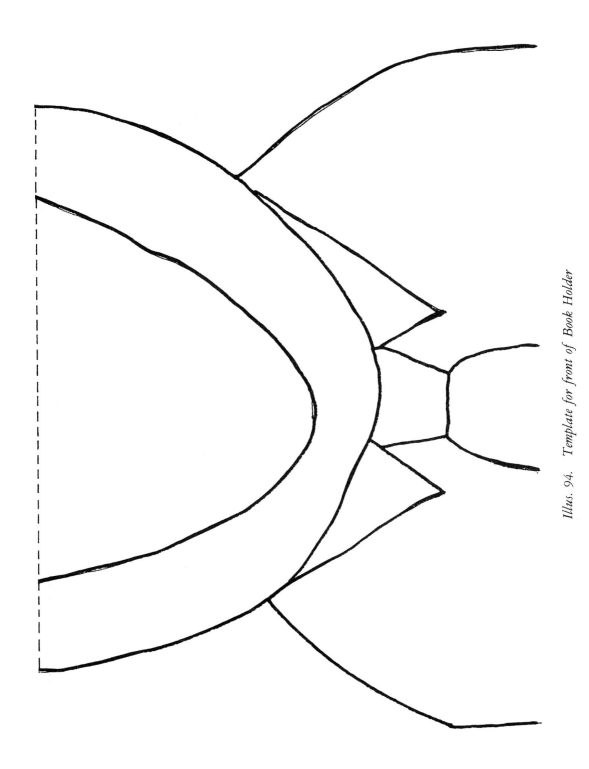

Illus. 94. Template for front of Book Holder

# Cat Pen Holder

My own children love drawing and coloring, and here is a simple, very practical way of storing soft-tip pens. They can see at a glance if any are missing when clearing up, and the lids can be jammed in the block so pens don't dry up prematurely!

## MATERIALS

Softwood, 1½" (40 mm) thick: 4" (100 mm) × 4¾" (120 mm)
Plywood, ¼" (6 mm) thick: 5" (127 mm) wide × 12" (305 mm) long
Enamel paints: yellow, red, black and white
2 small slotted wood screws

On the plywood, mark out the template of the cat (Illus. 96). The template is shortened: you should allow for the extra length by extending the two body lines 3" (75 mm) below the dashed line on the template. The cat outline is cut out using a fretsaw. Sand the edges with medium and then fine sandpaper.

Make sure that you have drawn on all the feature lines to act as a guide when painting. Varnish the outline of the cat and leave to dry.

*Illus. 95.*

The block is cut to size using a T-square to mark out, and cut using a backsaw. (A simple bench hook makes it easier.) Sand all the surfaces smooth with medium sandpaper. The drilling diagram (Illus. 97) is to scale; so you can either trace the position of the holes or measure them out. Four rows of ⅜" (10-mm) -diameter holes are drilled, each at an interval of ¾" (20 mm). Mark the center points for drilling clearly and carefully. Use tape around the drill bit 1" (25 mm) up as a makeshift depth gauge and drill to a depth of 1" (25 mm). Concentrate on keeping the drill upright.

*Illus. 96. Cat body template for Cat Pen Holder*

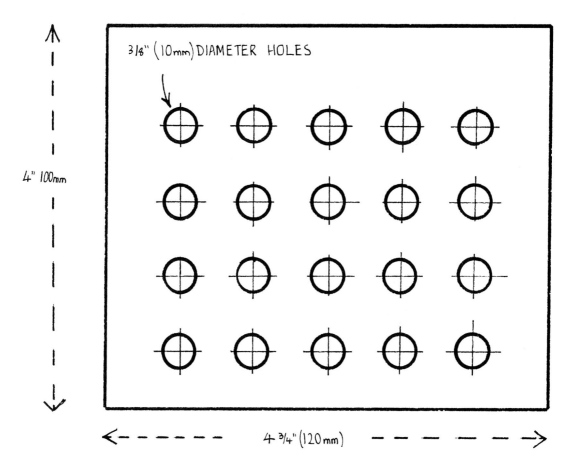

3/8" (10mm) DIAMETER HOLES

4" 100mm

4 3/4" (120 mm)

*Illus. 97.   Drilling diagram for base of Cat Pen Holder*

Sometimes even the sharpest drill bits will cause minor splinters as they begin the cut, but these little imperfections can be sanded off after drilling. Rub down the edges and surfaces with fine sandpaper, and then steel wool. Seal with varnish to protect the wood from the soft-tip ink!

I painted the cat outline when the pieces were still separate. The cat's fur markings were black gloss; whiskers—white; cat's eyes—yellow; nose—pink or red. Then when dry, I applied a final coat of varnish (Color Illus. A2).

When dry the cat outline is simply screwed from the nonpainted side (near the base) into the block using counter-sunk screws. Or, nail and glue it. The finished holder can be free standing, or hung on a nail to keep it away from the "wrong" hands.

Of course this simple idea can be extended to store different objects, using any outline shape you like, and by altering the hole sizes to suit.

*Illus. 98.*

# Old Boot Threading Toy

The skill of threading is needed for many activities in nursery school. This toy helps children to develop coordination and, of course, eventually to tie their own laces. There are two sets of holes on the toy. The smaller holes require more skill and are the same size as the lace holes on real shoes. You can design many other threading toys besides this one such as boards with patterns of holes, or blocks with holes to thread together to make snakes. They are all enjoyed by young children. The "Old Boot," like most threading toys, is easy and quick to make.

## MATERIALS

Plywood, ⅜″ (9 mm) thick: 8″ (200 mm) × 8¾″ (220 mm)
Quadrant moulding, ¾″ (20 mm) diameter: 13½″ (340 mm)
Finishing nails, 1″ (25 mm)
1 Football lace
1 Shoelace
Enamel paint: gold and black
Wood stain: dark brown
Glue

Start by tracing the boot outline (Illus. 100) on to the clean, smooth surface of the plywood. Mark the centers of the holes with the tip of a compass. Cut out the outline shape with a fretsaw and smooth all the edges carefully with fine sandpaper.

The large holes are ⅜ " (10 mm) in diameter and the smaller holes are ⅛ " (3 mm) in diameter; so you will need the appropriate drill bits. Plywood is quite difficult to drill through without some splitting as the drill exits the underside of the wood. To prevent this, clamp the boot shape down hard to a piece of scrap wood. Drill out all the holes, and then sand any rough edges.

To clean out the smaller holes I heated a nail (held in pliers) until red hot and scorched out the hole, to ensure that nothing snagged the little lace when in use!

Next decorate the boot outline. I used a dark wood stain and then varnished all the surfaces. When the varnish was dry, I drew on stitch lines with a thin brush

using black enamel paint and carefully ringed the holes with gold paint (Color Illus. A2).

Last, cut two pieces of ¾ " (20 mm) quadrant moulding, each 6¾ " (170 mm) long. They are glued and nailed to the base of the boot using 1" (25 mm) finishing nails (Illus. 99).

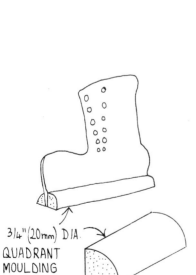

*Illus. 99. Old Boot assembly diagram*

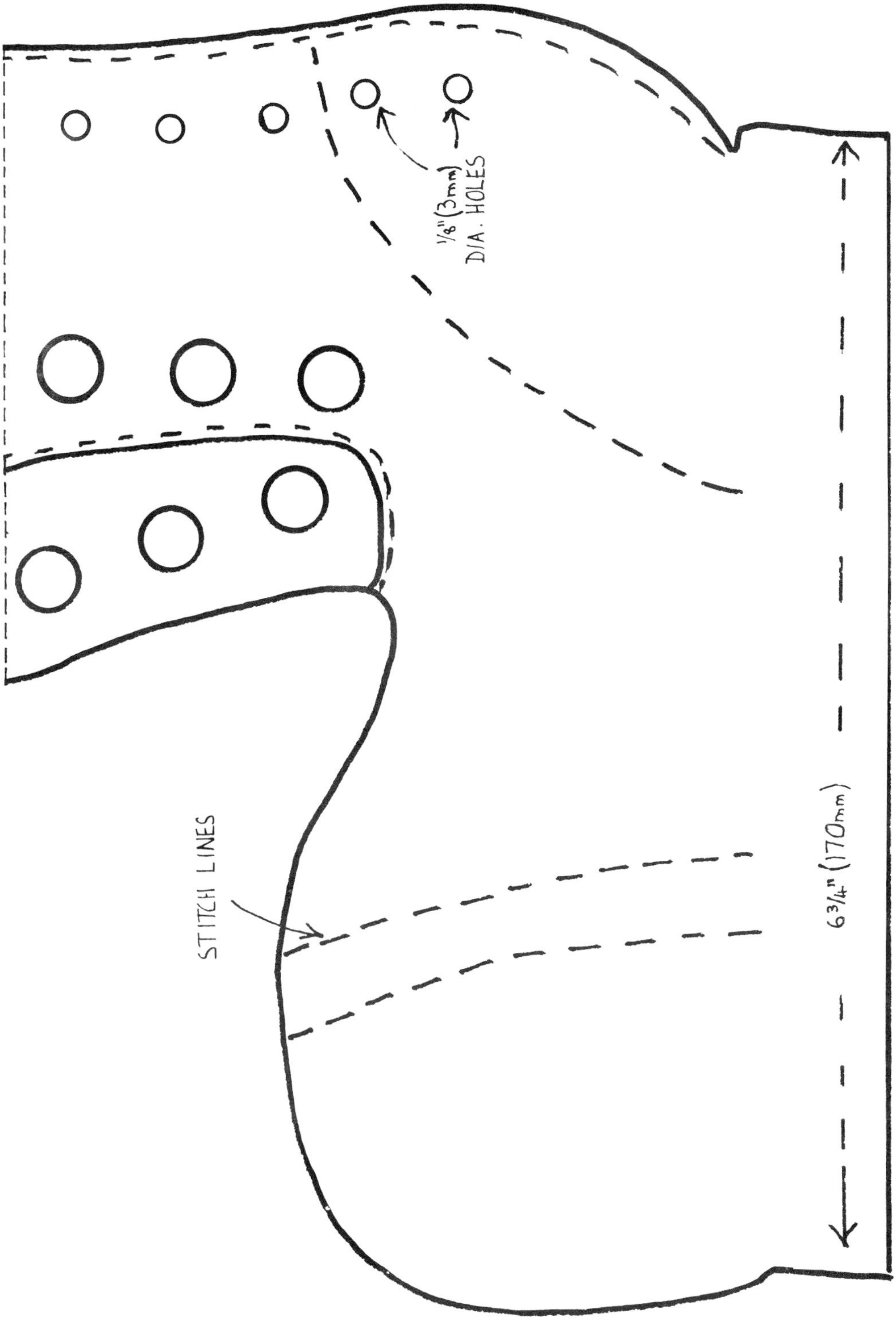

¹⁄₈" (3mm)
DIA. HOLES

STITCH LINES

6³⁄₄" (170mm)

*Illus. 100. Old Boot template and painting guide*

*Illus. 101.*

# Steamer Pencil Holder

This simple boat structure for holding pencils or soft-tip pens is made by gluing blocks onto a basic hull shape. It is made of softwood and left with a natural finish (Color Illus. A2). The colors of the different pencils contrast nicely with the natural wood. (I painted my prototype in bright colors and it didn't look as nice.)

## MATERIALS

Softwood, 1¾″ (45 mm) thick: 2¾″ (70 mm) wide × 16″ (410 mm) long for the hull
Softwood, ¾″ (20 mm) thick: 2″ (50 mm) wide × 5″ (130 mm) long for the bridge and deckhouse blocks
Softwood, ¾″ (20 mm) thick: 2¾″ (70 mm) × 3″ (76 mm) for the forecastle block

Dowel, ¾″ (20 mm) diameter: 1″ (25 mm) long for the funnel
6 small upholstery tacks for portholes

First cut the hull block to length and mark out the cutting lines (Illus. 102) to form the triangular shape of the bow: begin by drawing a guideline across the width of the deck 1½″ (40 mm) from one end of the block. Connect the two endpoints to the center point of the edge with straight lines, to form the pointed shape. With a backsaw cut vertically down on the waste side of the lines, so that you end up with an even-sided, pointed bow.

At the other end of the block, mark a line across the width of the deck ¾″ (20 mm) in from the end and draw an even curve with a compass connecting the two end points to form the rounded stern.

Use a backsaw and cut tangent "slices" on the waste side of the curve to form a roughly rounded rear end to the boat. Use a flat file to take away any roughness on the stern and bow.

Next mark out the deck with the positions of the centers for the ⅜" (10-mm)-diameter holes. Draw two parallel lines ¾" (20 mm) in from each deck side and space the hole centers out, so that they are an inch (25 mm) apart. Drill the holes out using a ⅜" (10 mm) drill bit. Use a strip of masking tape wrapped round the drill 1" (25 mm) up from the tip as a depth gauge so that you get each hole 1" (25 mm) deep. Try to keep the drill upright so that the pencils will be vertical when stored in the holes.

Now, carefully cut out the two blocks for the deckhouse and bridge. The deckhouse is 2½" (64 mm) × 2" (50 mm) × ¾" (20 mm) and the bridge block is 2" (50 mm) × 1¾" (45 mm) × ¾" (20 mm). Sand the edges smooth to clean up the end grain but don't round the edges and corners too much. Tap three small upholstery tacks in each side of the deck-house in line to suggest portholes. If children are young or might pull them out, paint on small porthole circles.

The forecastle block can be marked out by placing the block of ¾" (20 mm) wood under the bow and drawing around the bow to give you an accurate shape to glue in place. Cut it to a length of 3" (76 mm) and drill the two ⅜" (10 mm) pencil holes. Cut the bow lines with a back-saw, or use a coping saw if you have slightly curved your bows.

Glue the deckhouse in place and glue the bridge to the deckhouse and the deck. Glue the forecastle block in place as well. Wipe away any excess glue with a damp cloth. When dry give the boat its final sanding, paying particular attention to the bows and the rounded stern. Try to erase all saw marks and scratches!

Finally, cut the dowel funnel and glue it in place. Seal the entire boat in varnish. It is a good idea to give the deck several coats so that clumsily replaced soft-tip pens don't permanently spoil the natural wood finish.

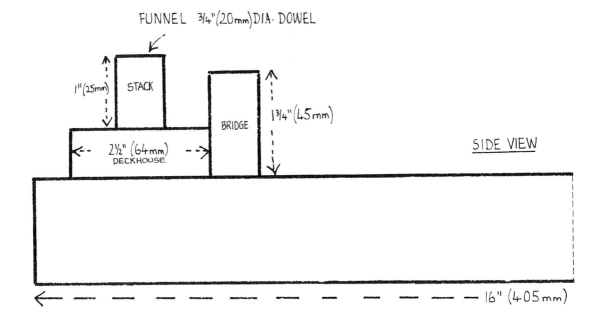

FUNNEL 3/4"(20mm) DIA· DOWEL

STACK

1"(25mm)

BRIDGE

1 3/4"(45mm)

SIDE VIEW

2½" (64mm)
DECKHOUSE

16" (405mm)

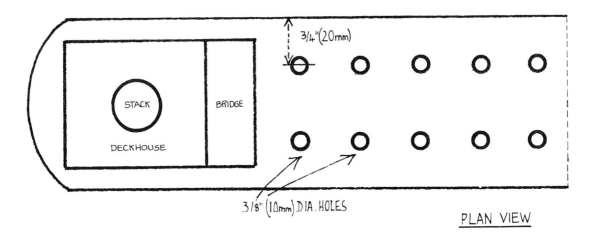

3/4"(20mm)

STACK

BRIDGE

DECKHOUSE

3/8" (10mm) DIA. HOLES

PLAN VIEW

*Illus. 102.   Steamer Pencil Holder templates,
side view (top) and plan view (bottom)*

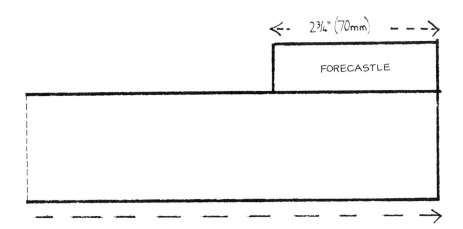

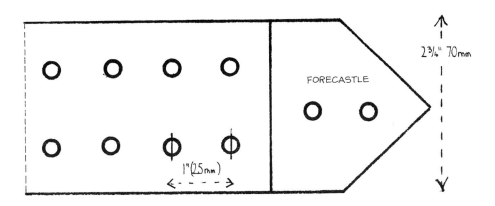

*Illus. 102 (continued)*

*Illus. 103.*

## House Picture Frame

Children love photographs of the family and here is a novel way to display them. This design was taken from a scaled-up photograph of our old house which I transferred onto plywood. The windows are cut out with a fretsaw and the colors follow the original decoration of the house. Using thin strips of wood on the reverse, a recess is made to take a sheet of glass or Plexiglas, and photographs are carefully selected and positioned on cardboard, to make it look as though little people are in the house.

## MATERIALS

Plywood, ¼″ (6 mm) thick: 10¼″ (260 mm) × 14½″ (365 mm)

Softwood, ½″ (13 mm) thick: ½″ (13 mm) × 48″ (1220 mm) long

Hardboard: approximately 10″ (255 mm) × 12″ (305 mm)

Glass or Plexiglas

Finishing nails: ⅝″ (15 mm)

2 small screw eyes

Strong cord

Cardboard

Begin by cleaning and sanding smooth the plywood surface using fine-grade sandpaper in the direction of the grain on the surface veneer. Transfer the design (Illus. 104) on to a large sheet of thin, plain paper. Tape two sheets of flexible carbon paper, carbon face down, on the plywood with masking tape, so that your plywood is covered. Then place your drawing carefully over the plywood and tape in position.

Go over the outline of the house and all the features (using a ruler where necessary) with a sharp H.B. grade pencil. Remove the drawing and the carbons carefully. You should now have a perfect picture of the house on the plywood. The carbon lines are less easily erased than mere pencil lines and will enable you to clean the surface if necessary at a later stage without disappearing.

Use a fretsaw to cut out the roof line and the outline shape of the house (although a backsaw may be used to cut the straight edges more quickly and accurately). Sand the edges smooth with medium, then fine sandpaper.

The next step is to cut out the windows. Here you will need to load and unload the fretsaw many times, because you need to pierce each window rectangle with a fine drill (or you can tap through with a brad) to enable you to feed the fretsaw blade through the plywood. Since the house is quite large, and the "throat" of the fretsaw restricts some of the cuts you need to make, you'll find that you sometimes have to pierce the window rectangles in more than one place to enable you to cut out completely.

Take care to cut along the edges of the window sashes (glazing bars) very carefully and accurately. It is quite a long job to cut all the windows out, but the end effect is lovely!

Having cut out all the window rectangles and the door glass, the next stage is to carefully sand the inner edges of the windows, so that they are neat, splinter free (and easier to paint later) and as straight as possible. (I used fine-grade sandpaper wrapped over a thin, small flat file to get rid of the irregularities in my cutting.)

You should now have a house "skeleton" that resembles the front of a doll's house! Now you need to make the recess which will take the glass or Plexiglas and the hardboard backing. This is simply achieved by cutting the thin strips of ½″ (6-mm)-square wood to length and nailing and gluing them in position around the perimeter of the house on the reverse side (Illus. 105). The strips are flush with the edge of the "house."

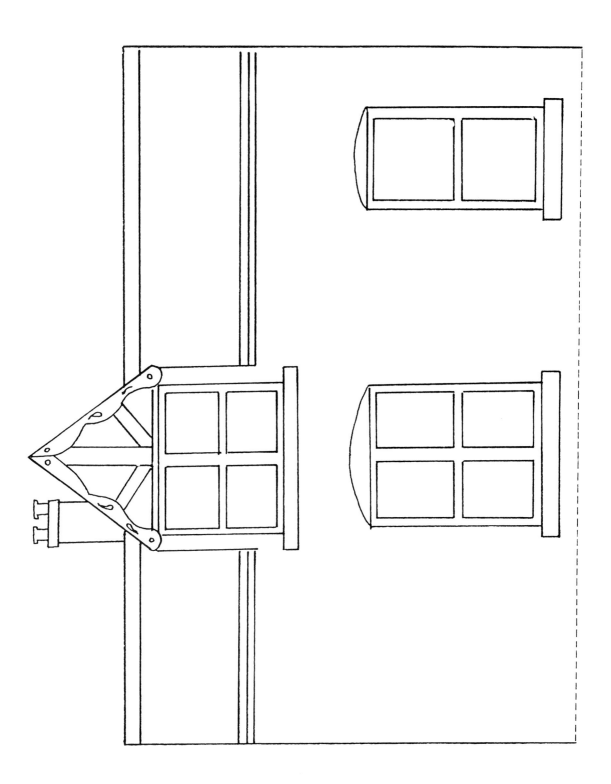

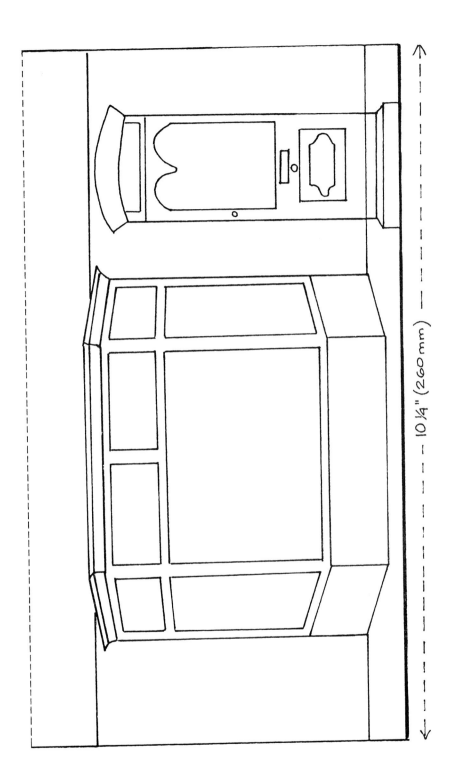

Illus. 104.  House Picture Frame template

10¼" (260 mm)

Cut out a piece of hardboard which fits easily and neatly into the recess. You should also cut out a piece of thin cardboard to the same size on which you can later mount the selected photographs in their precise positions. Glass or Plexiglas can be ordered to size, but if you use glossy photographs you can manage without either.

To decorate the house, first you should seal the entire front surface with a clear varnish. Don't forget the inside edges of the windows. I used remnants of the actual colors used to paint the house. The door was left "natural wood" and the window sashes painted green, except for the bottom bay window. Tile grey was used for the slate roof, and brick red for the ridge tiles and brickwork (Color Illus. C2).

When the paints are dry, reverse the house and screw the screw eyes into the outside edges of the recess strips about two-thirds of the way up. Tie the thin strong cord to the eyes, to hang the frame.

Use finishing nails to hold in the hardboard backing when your photographs are in place.

Why not use this idea to make a frame in the shape of your own house? Make a scale drawing of your house that has dimensions roughly similar to my example. (Too big and it will be hard to fret out the windows. Too small and the little window frames won't do your photographs justice.) You could work from a color slide of the front view of your house and project it onto a large sheet of white paper. Move the projector to get the image the size you want and simply draw over the lines.

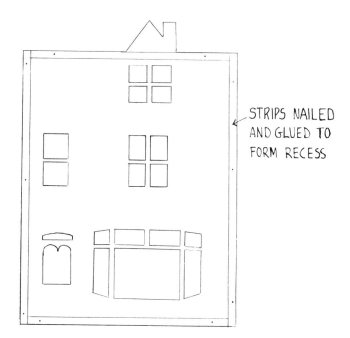

STRIPS NAILED AND GLUED TO FORM RECESS

*Illus. 105.   Construction details, reverse of house*

# Stacking and
# Counting Toys

## Stacking Tower

This very simple toy is always popular with young toddlers. It gives them the pleasure of stacking made easy. They seem to love threading on the rings time and again. Of course it also helps them to practise the vital early skill of hand/eye coordination.

### MATERIALS
Pine or plywood, ¾″ (20 mm) thick: 5″ (125 mm) × 5″ (125 mm) for the base
Pine or plywood, ¼″ (6 mm) thick: 54″ (1375 mm) × 4″ (76 mm) to make 18 discs
Dowel, ½″ (13 mm) diameter: 9″ (230 mm) long

*Illus. 106.*

**Base.** Draw a circle 5″ (125 mm) in diameter on the square of ¾″ (20 mm) pine or plywood. Clearly mark the center of the circle as it is the location for centering the drill when you drill out to position the dowel rod.

With a coping saw, carefully cut out the circle. Do not cut too close to the edge of the circle, and cut on the "waste" side of the line. Sand the edges with coarse, medium and then fine sandpaper to get a perfect circle. (You may find it easier to wrap the sandpaper over a flat file to get more pressure.)

Cut the dowel rod to a 9″ (230 mm) length and smooth one of the ends. Next drill out the center of the base. A ½″ (13-mm)-flat bit in an electric drill will make the job a lot easier! Take care to keep the drill upright. Glue the rough

end of the dowel into the base (Illus. 108) and wipe away the excess glue with a damp cloth.

**Discs.** These are cut out from ¼″ (6 mm) plywood or pine. Simply draw out 18 circles of 1½″ (38 mm) radius (Illus. 107), marking the center of each circle clearly with the compass point. Cut out either with a fretsaw or coping saw on the waste side of the wood. Before drilling, sand the edges to get a neat circle, and clamp each disc on to a piece of waste wood, so that the drill doesn't split the wood as it penetrates the underside of the disc.

The discs have to have a slightly enlarged center hole, so that they fit easily over the dowel rod. To do this use a rattail file, or a pencil or thin dowel wrapped with a small piece of sandpaper.

I made my discs out of pine and stained nine of them green all over and left the other nine natural wood color (Color Illus. A1). Varnish the surfaces of the discs when cleaned up. Of course you could paint patterns on them in enamel paints if you wanted to!

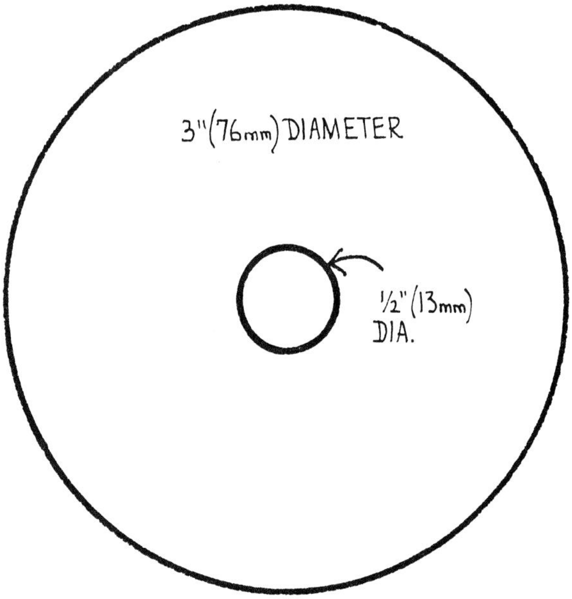

3″(76mm) DIAMETER

½″(13mm) DIA.

*Illus. 107.   Disc template*

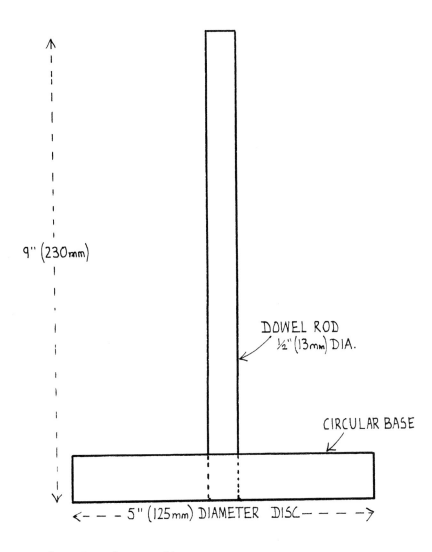

9" (230mm)

DOWEL ROD
½" (13mm) DIA.

CIRCULAR BASE

<— — — 5" (125mm) DIAMETER DISC— — — —>

*Illus. 108.   Stacking Tower base assembly diagram*

*Illus. 109.*

# Stacking Caterpillar

The 16 segments of this toy are held together on a dowel rod which is glued in to the tail segment. When put together, the dowel rod forms the nose on the face segment (Illus. 109 and 110). Children either stack the pieces on the dowel to form the animal, or they can line up the separated pieces domino style and set off a chain reaction, knocking them all over!

## MATERIALS

Softwood, ½″ (13 mm) thick: 3½″ (90 mm) × 48″ (1220 mm)
Dowel, ½″ (13 mm) diameter: 12″ (305 mm) long

To make the toy, drilling of the center holes must be accurate so that the pieces line up nicely when held together on the

rod. A pillar drill attachment to an electric drill makes the job easier.

First, make a cardboard template from the solid lines on the body segment pattern (Illus. 111), and carefully mark out 14 pieces on the wood.

Pay particular attention to marking the center point for the dowel rod hole by passing a compass point through your cardboard template and marking the wood underneath. Remember to leave a small gap between each segment drawing on your wood to allow for a saw cut as you separate the segments before cutting them more carefully with a coping saw.

Mark out the feeler segment (Illus. 112) and the face segment (Illus. 113) by copying the solid lines from the two diagrams. Mark the pieces on the wood and cut

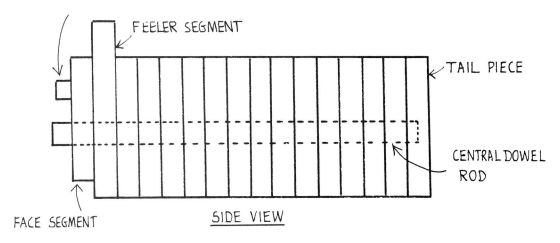

DOWEL EYES
GLUED IN PLACE

FEELER SEGMENT

TAIL PIECE

CENTRAL DOWEL
ROD

FACE SEGMENT

SIDE VIEW

*Illus. 110.   Stacking Caterpillar assembly
diagram*

them out with the coping saw. Each segment should be sanded to shape with coarse- and medium-grade sandpaper, but wait until you have drilled out the center holes and lined all the pieces up on the dowel rod before final sanding.

Drill out each segment center hole very carefully and accurately. If you haven't got a pillar-drill attachment, or can't borrow one, and if you have no one to watch and guide you to get the drill vertical, you can always make adjustments to the hole diameter at a later stage to allow for slight errors!

Cut the dowel rod to length, having threaded all the pieces on to it, and allow for the nose to stick out beyond the face. Mark off and, after removing the segments, cut the rod with a backsaw, taking care not to split it.

Glue one end of the dowel rod into the tail section and wipe off the excess glue. Check that it will dry in a vertical position. Give the other parts their final sanding and decorate. I used green stain for the face and alternate segments as in Color Illus. A1. (I should have stained the face before I glued on the dowel eyes!) Varnish when dry to seal.

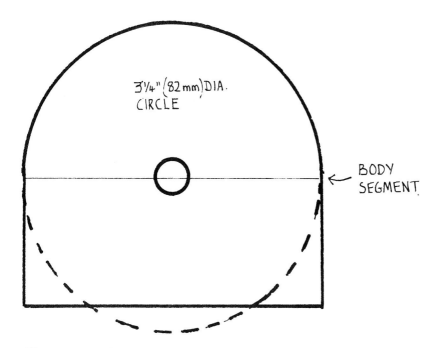

3¼" (82mm) DIA.
CIRCLE

← BODY SEGMENT

*Illus. 111.   Body segment*

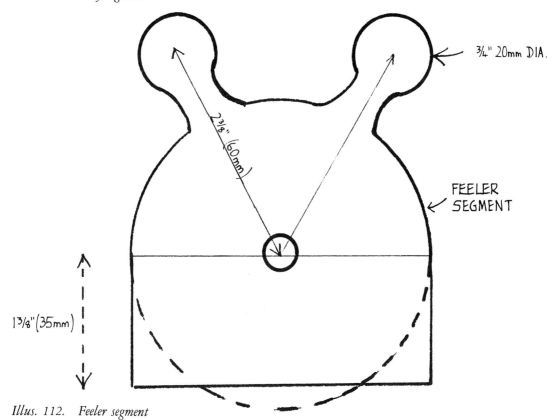

¾" 20mm DIA.

2³⁄₈" (60mm)

FEELER SEGMENT

1³⁄₈" (35mm)

*Illus. 112.   Feeler segment*

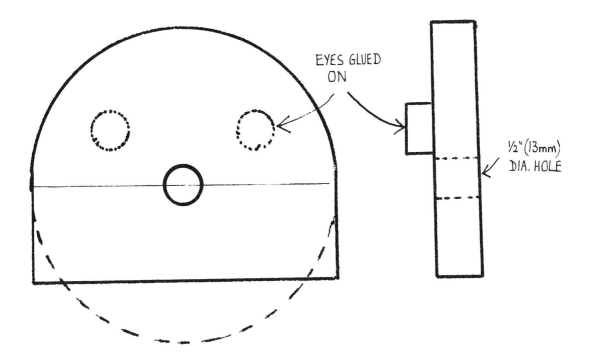

EYES GLUED ON

½" (13mm) DIA. HOLE

*Illus. 113.   Face segment*

*Illus. 114.*

# "Last Out" Pegboard Game

This simple game has two functions. It consists of a softwood base with 18 holes arranged in rows, which take little people made from wooden clothespins (clothes pegs), as shown in Illus. 114. Younger children enjoy posting objects in holes, and since the pins are painted with a different color for each row, they can arrange them in the correct color family. Older children can play the game of "last out." The rules are simple to learn. Each player can remove any number of pegs from one row during their turn. The object of the game is to leave your opponent with the last peg.

## MATERIALS
Softwood, ¾″ (20 mm) thick: 8″ (203 mm) × 10″ (253 mm)
18 wooden clothespins
Enamel paints: 5 different colors

With the rectangle of ¾″ (20-mm)-thick softwood mark out the pyramid arrangement of drill centers (Illus. 115). (I cut mine from a scrap of 8″ window sill, which has one edge rounded.)

The bottom row should be marked out first. Draw a light guideline parallel to a 10″ (250 mm) edge, 2″ (50 mm) in. Find the center of your guideline and mark the center for the first of the seven holes. Each center is spaced 1¼″ (30 mm) apart. Each row is 1⅜″ (35 mm) apart.

Having marked on the centers, drill out the holes using a ½″ (13 mm) drill bit to a depth of ½″ (13 mm). Sand the edges and surfaces of the board. Clean off and seal with varnish.

Next select 18 wooden clothespins and cut them each to a length of 2½″ (65 mm). The quality of these pegs varies: some are rougher in finish than others; so they should be sanded with medium and fine sandpaper to make a good foundation for decorating. When clean and smooth, check that each peg fits in the hole. You may need to tailor them by sanding to make them easy to place and remove. Draw the face on the "head" of the peg with a fine drawing pen. Seal with varnish. Choose a different color for the pegs in each row. Paint the body with enamel paint, and apply a second coat when dry (Color Illus. A1).

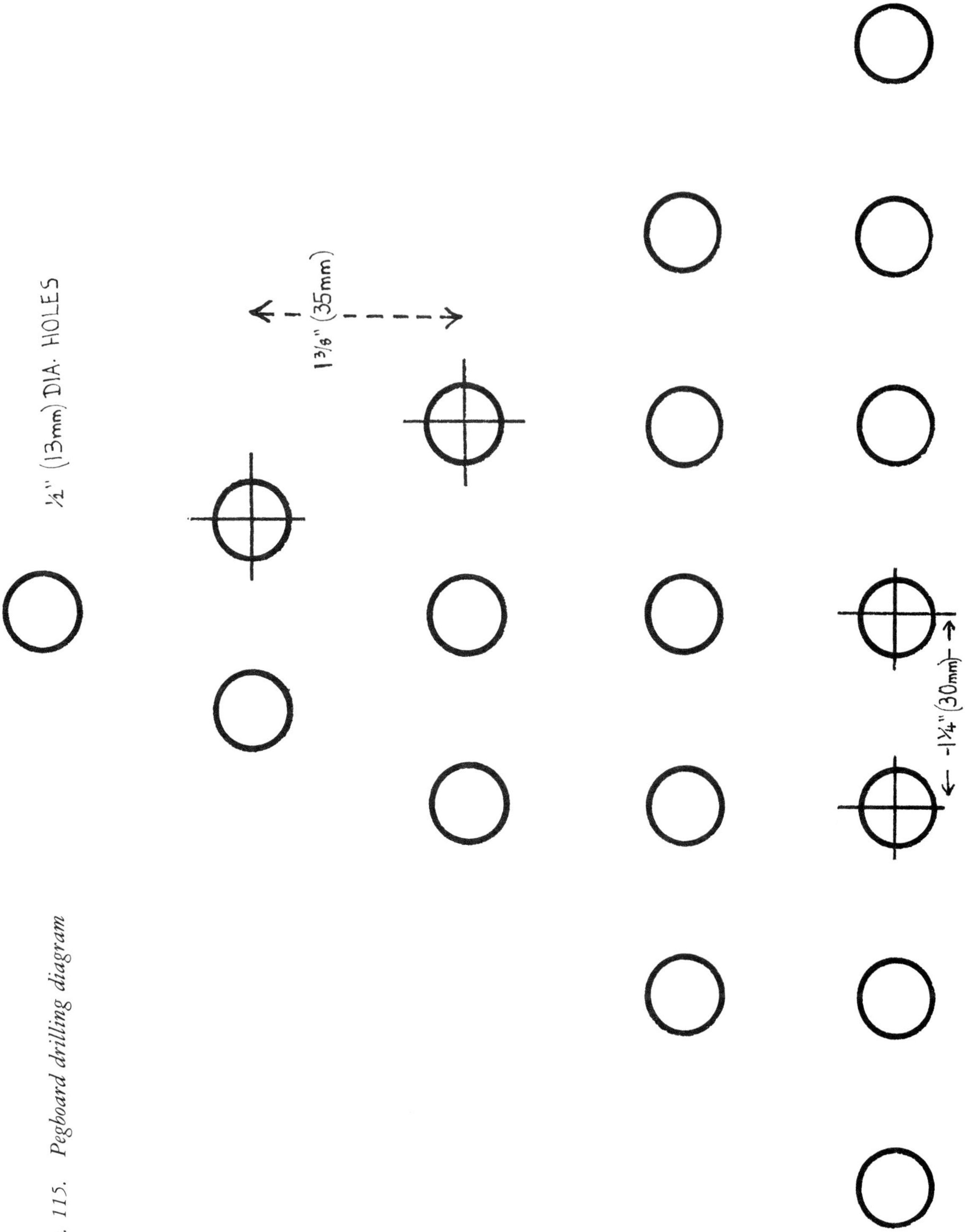

*Illus. 115. Pegboard drilling diagram*

½" (13mm) DIA. HOLES

1³⁄₈" (35mm)

1¼" (30mm)

*Illus. 116.*

# Counting Tree

This toy makes an attractive addition to any playroom. Fruit-shaped pieces of wood are hung on little hooks on a tree background. Younger children simply enjoy removing and replacing the fruit. Slightly older children will also enjoy trying to match the numbers on the fruit with those on the tree; so the game is helpful in teaching youngsters to recognize numbers.

## MATERIALS

Plywood, ⅜″ (9 mm) thick: 12½″ (320 mm) × 15″ (380 mm) to cut out the tree shape

Plywood, ½″ (13 mm) thick: 7″ (180 mm) × 7″ (180 mm) to make the circular base

Softwood, 8″ (220 mm) in length: 1½″ (40 mm) to make the trunk support

Plywood or softwood, ¼″ (6 mm) thick: 2″ (50 mm) × 24″ (610 mm) to cut out 10 fruit shapes

10 small screw eyes and screw hooks

Countersunk slotted wood screw: 1¼″ (32 mm)

Lost-head brads: ½″ (13 mm)

Rub-on numbers

Prepare the parts of the tree, following the instructions for the Bird Display Tree on pages 68–72.

**Fruit.** Choose apples or pears, and make a thin cardboard template from Illus. 117. Each fruit is hung on the tree on a small screw hook. The screw eye is screwed in place where the stem would be on the real fruit. Screwing into the end grain is inadvisable for safety reasons, as the eye would pull out easily. So when you draw around your template, position the shape on the wood so that the eye can be screwed across the grain.

Cut out ten wooden fruits using a fretsaw, and smooth the edges. If you want to make the job more simple you could slice a 1¼″ (32-mm)-diameter dowel rod to make cherries! Screw in the eyes to the top edge of each fruit.

Varnish each fruit to seal, or apply an appropriate undercoat. I used gloss enamel (red for the apples, yellow for the pears).

**Finishing.** The tree trunk is stained dark brown, and the front and back of the tree are stained green. The circular base is also stained green. When the stain has dried, mark the position for each hook, then apply white rub-on numbers next to them. Dab varnish on each number. Apply the numbers to each of the fruits. I used rub-on numbers because I wanted the shape of the number on the fruit to match that on the tree. You could, of course, paint your numbers on freehand using a fine paintbrush. See Color Illus. A1.

The last job is to seal the tree with varnish and screw the little hooks in place.

After making these little trees, I made a larger version with 20 apples. The method of construction was exactly the same, but the dimensions obviously were bigger. I made the base disc 10″ (255 mm) in diameter and the tree 22″ (560 mm) high and 19″ (480 mm) wide at the widest point. I drew my larger tree shape freehand onto the plywood.

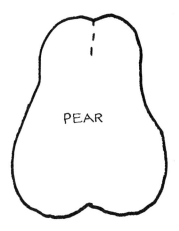

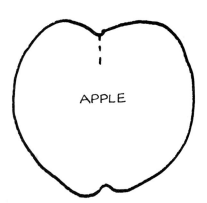

*Illus. 117. Fruit templates for Counting Tree*

*Illus. 118.*

# Counting Loaf

This toy helps young children learn the concept of numbers. It is in the shape of a loaf of bread and is composed of slices of wood held together by a concealed dowel rod (Illus. 118). Each slice has a printed number and that number of holes. Children place short dowel pegs in these holes and learn to associate the number with the quantity it represents.

## MATERIALS

Softwood, ¾″ (20 mm) thick: 3″ (76 mm) wide × 42″ (1065 mm) long to make the slices

Dowel, ¼″ (6 mm) diameter: 96″ (2440 mm) long
Dark wood stain

First, use a T-square and mark off ten "slices," each 4″ (102 mm) wide, allowing for the width of the backsaw cut. Use a backsaw to cut out the ten pieces.

Next, copy Illus. 119 to make a cardboard template and carefully mark on the template the position of the centers for drilling the holes. Place the template over each slice in turn and draw around the template.

Illus. 120 shows how you should mark each of the 10 slices. The arrangement of

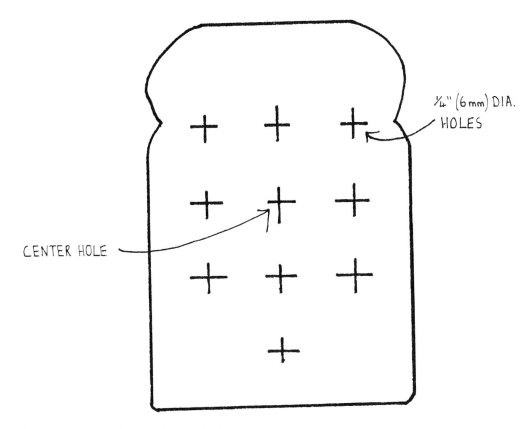

CENTER HOLE

¼" (6 mm) DIA. HOLES

*Illus. 119.   Bread slice template with drill centers*

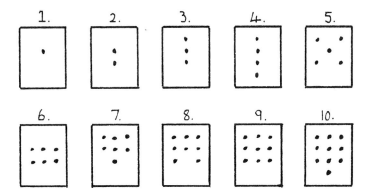

*Illus. 120.   Layout of holes to be drilled*

the holes allows for the center hole to be in the same position on each slice, because the dowel rod that holds the loaf together must pass through each slice in a straight line, with the exception of the "crust" ends. The first and last slice have the center hole drilled only part way through, so that the center dowel is concealed when all the slices are put together on it.

The drilling of the center hole is fairly critical if the loaf is to line up neatly. If you have no pillar drill attachment, it may help to drill the first slice; then clamp the next slice accurately to the first one and use the original hole to guide the subsequent one.

Use a drill of a slightly larger diameter than ¼" (6 mm), so that the dowels fit easily and the pegs can be removed and replaced easily. Drill each slice after marking the centers of the holes through the cardboard template with a compass point or nail.

Remember that the two slices that form the crust ends are not drilled right through, but only to a depth of ½" (13 mm). Drill to the same shallow depth for all the peg holes that will hold the little pegs.

Take the eight slices that are drilled through and line them up on a 7" (177 mm) length of the ¼" (6-mm)-diameter dowel rod and check that the loaf sits flat. Put on the crust ends and check their alignment.

Use a coping saw to shape the top edges of each slice. Sand the edges with sandpaper, paying special attention to the end grain.

Next carefully stain the *edges* of each slice with a dark wood stain using a fine paint brush to make the "crust," taking care not to stain the inside white portion (Illus. 118 and Color Illus. A1). Rub down the flat surfaces with fine-grade sandpaper. Apply the rub-on numbers on each slice at the top as shown on the template diagram. Dab varnish over the numbers and then apply a sealing coat to the "white bread" surfaces.

The last job is to cut out 55 little dowel pegs. Each will have a length of 1" (25 mm). Sand each one with medium and fine sandpaper to smooth any roughness after cutting.

# Action Toys and Games

*Illus. 121.*

## Tractor

This simple little toy tractor is both a vehicle that moves and a little puzzle. I'm glad I didn't get around to gluing the wheels on because one day my son Jack pulled it apart and enjoyed putting it together again and again.

The tractor project demonstrates the principle of how to make wheeled pull- or push-along toys. For example, the elephant on page 79 could be put on wheels as a pull-along toy. Accurate drilling is the key to making toy wheeled vehicles.

## MATERIALS

Softwood, ¾″ (20 mm) thick: 1½″ (39 mm) × 3½″ (90 mm) for the body
Dowel, ⅛″ (3 mm) diameter: 6″ (154 mm) long for the axles and exhaust stack
Dowel, 1″ (25 mm) diameter for the small wheels
Dowel, 1¾″ (45 mm) diameter for the large wheels
1 wooden clothespin

**Body.** First trace the outline of the tractor body (Illus. 120) on to the softwood and cut out the shape carefully with a coping saw. Mark on the positions of the axle-hole drill centers with a compass point. Drill out the two axle holes using a ⅛″ (3 mm) drill. Be extra careful to keep the drill upright or the wheels will wobble eccentrically when put on the axles.

Now spend a little time concentrating on carefully sanding the edges of the body. On such a small toy success depends on a good finish.

The next step is to drill the hole for the driver and the exhaust pipe. On the top edge of the tractor body, mark the two positions indicated in Illus. 123. Hold the tractor body in a vise and drill vertically into the top edge. The hole for the driver is ½″ (13 mm) in diameter, and the exhaust hole is ⅛″ (3 mm) in diameter.

**Axles.** Cut the axles to length next. The front axle is 1¾″ (45 mm), and the rear axle is 2¼″ (57 mm) long. They are cut from ⅛″ (3-mm)-diameter dowel.

**Wheels.** You could use off-cuts of plywood of the appropriate thickness, draw out circles and cut them out with a fretsaw, then sand them down. However, slicing dowel rod is quicker and easier. Mark off the dowel rod. The front wheels are ⅜″ (10 mm) thick, and the rear wheels are ¾″ (20 mm) thick. Use a mitre block to slice the dowel (Illus. 122) if you don't trust the accuracy of your cutting with a backsaw. Sand each sawn surface by rubbing the wheel on a sheet of me-

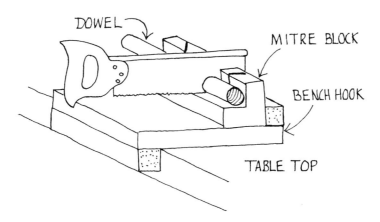

*Illus. 122. Cutting out wheels*

PLAN VIEW

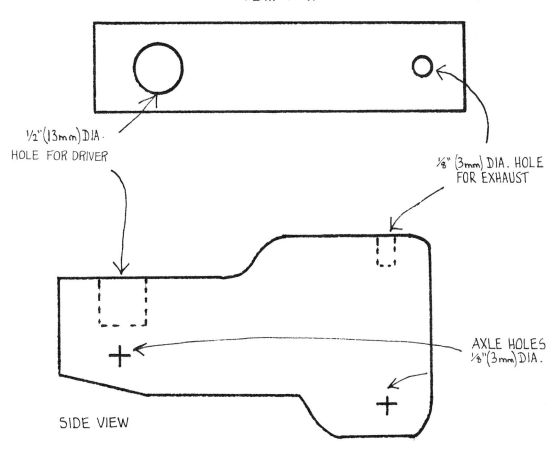

½"(13mm)DIA.
HOLE FOR DRIVER

⅛" (3mm) DIA. HOLE
FOR EXHAUST

AXLE HOLES
⅛"(3mm)DIA.

SIDE VIEW

*Illus. 123.   Tractor template, plan view (top)
and side view (bottom)*

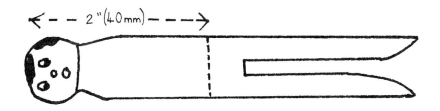

←  - - 2"(40mm) - - - →

*Illus. 124.   Clothespin driver*

dium-grade sandpaper laid on a flat, smooth surface.

Mark the center point of each wheel by drawing a diameter line across the widest part of the disc. Measure along your line to find the center. Drill the ⅛ ″ (3 mm) hole carefully and vertically.

**Exhaust Stack.** This is cut from ⅛ ″ (3-mm)-diameter dowel to a 1″ (25 mm) length. To make things a little more interesting I tightened the little dowel into my electric drill chuck, gripped the handle of my drill in my woodworking vise and used the drill as a little lathe by applying sandpaper to the dowel tip as the drill turned the dowel.

**Driver.** The driver is simply a clothespin, cut to a length of 2″ (51 mm) with a fretsaw (Illus. 124). Clothespins are made of beechwood; so if you sand the surface of the peg with fine sandpaper and then use steel wool, you get a lovely finish. Draw the little face and clothes on the driver with a fine soft-tip pen and dab over the lines with varnish. You may have to sand the "legs" to make the driver fit easily into his hole.

Varnish the cleaned-up tractor body. I painted the wheels red with gloss enamel paint after sealing with varnish (Color Illus. D2). I didn't glue the wheels to the axles, but if you do, put a small dab of glue inside each axle hole in the wheel, having ensured that the dowel axle itself moves freely in the hole in the tractor body. I screwed a hook into the back of the tractor for towing toy cars.

*Illus. 125.*

# Simple Racing Cars

The shape of these simple little cars is based on the shape of the old racing cars I played with as a child. They are quick and easy to make; so why not make several?

## MATERIALS

Softwood, ¾″ (20 mm) thick: 1½″ (40 mm) × 5″ (127 mm)
Dowel, 3/16″ (4 mm) diameter: 4″ (100 mm) long for axles
Dowel, 1″ (25 mm) diameter: 2″ (50 mm) long for the wheels
1 wooden clothespin
Enamel paints

The first step is to trace out the outline of the car body (Illus. 126) on to the softwood. The underside of the car is a straight line; so when copying the shape on the wood, place the bottom of the outline on an edge of the wood. Mark the position of the two hole centers to be drilled to take the axles.

With a coping saw, cut out the outline of the car, trying to keep the blade vertical. Next, drill out the axle holes. You need to use a drill bit with a slightly larger diameter than the little dowel axles, which have to move in the holes if the car is to "go." I used a ¼″ (6-mm)-diameter drill. Remember to place a piece of scrap wood underneath as you drill.

The next step is to drill the hole which takes the clothespin driver. The position of the hole is shown in the plan view of Illus. 126. I used a ½″ (13 mm) flat bit and drilled the hole to a depth of about ½″ (13 mm).

Now, using sandpaper, smooth the edges and other surfaces to get rid of the roughness caused by the coping-saw blade, and

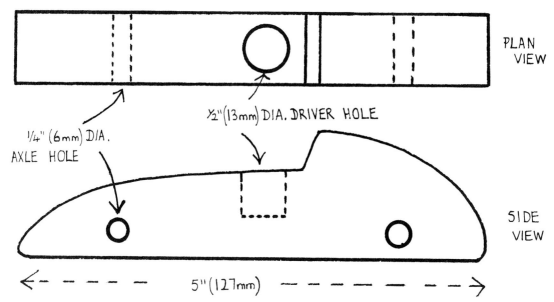

PLAN VIEW

½"(13mm) DIA. DRIVER HOLE

¼" (6mm) DIA. AXLE HOLE

SIDE VIEW

5"(127mm)

*Illus. 126.   Racing car template, plan view (top) and side view (bottom)*

round off the edges. Finish off by using fine-grade sandpaper and rubbing with the grain.

The wheels are made in the same manner as the tractor wheels (above). Slice the 1″ (25-mm)-diameter dowel rod into ½″ (13-mm)-wide pieces, using a backsaw and holding the dowel rod either on a bench hook or mitre box. Try and get the sawn edges parallel. Rub the rough surfaces with sandpaper and round off the edges to remove any roughness. Mark the center of the wheel and drill the ³⁄₁₆″ (4 mm) holes, which should hold the axles securely. If you don't get the holes in the wheels in the exact center, the car will wobble when it is racing! Cut two dowel axles 2″ (50 mm) long from the 3/16″ (25-mm)-diameter dowel rod.

The driver is made by cutting the head end of the clothespin to a length of 1″ (25 mm). You will have to reduce the diameter a little so that the driver fits in the hole.

Seal the car body with varnish or undercoat and paint with bright enamel colors. I painted the wheels a complementary primary color and made the driver's helmet the same color as the tires. The clothespin driver's face and helmet were drawn on with a fine soft-tip or drawing pen. Then the driver was sealed with varnish, and the helmet painted when the sealer was dry (Color Illus. D2).

Finally, glue the driver in the "cockpit," insert the axles and fit on the wheels. There should be a small clearance between the wheels and the car body, so that the wheels don't drag as the car is "racing." I found that the axles were tight enough in the wheels not to need glue, but you can of course apply a little glue in each axle hole in the wheel just in case.

*Illus. 127.*

# Plane

On this little plane the wheels spin, the propeller spins, and the pilot can be removed; so it has lots of play value.

## MATERIALS

Plywood, ⅛″ (3 mm) thick: 3″ (75 mm) × 7½″ (190 mm) for the wings, tail plane and rudder

Plywood or hardwood, ⅛″ (3 mm) thick: ¾″ (20 mm) × 3″ (75 mm) for the propeller

Plywood, ⅜″ (10 mm) thick: 2″ (51 mm) × 2″ (51 mm) for the undercarriage support

1″ (25-mm)-diameter dowel for the wheels

Softwood, ¾″ (20 mm) thick: 2″ (51 mm) × 7″ (180 mm) for the fuselage

1 small screw eye, for the tail wheel

3 small cup washers, for wheel and propeller screws

3 wood screws, brass slotted (size 6): ¾″ (20 mm) long

1 brass screw, dome headed (size 6): 1½″ (13 mm)

**Wing, Tail Plane and Rudder.** Trace out the outline shapes of the wing, tail plane and rudder (Illus. 128) onto the ⅛″ (3 mm) plywood, and cut out with a fretsaw. (You can also use a utility knife and a steel rule to cut this thin plywood.) Smooth and round the edges with medium and then fine sandpaper, taking special care to smooth the thin edges so that successful painting can be achieved later.

**Propeller.** Next trace out the outline shape of the propeller (Illus. 129) on ⅛″

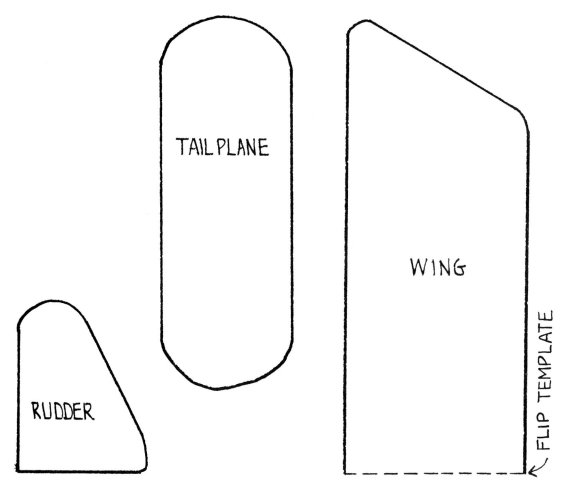

*Illus. 128.   Rudder, tail plane and wing*

(3 mm) plywood and drill out the screw hole, using a drill of a slightly larger diameter than the wood screw. This is to ensure that it spins freely when secured to the nose of the plane. (I used a lath of knot-free white hardwood instead of plywood to add a little strength to the propeller.) Smooth off the edges with sandpaper.

**Undercarriage Support.** Carefully mark out Illus. 130 on good-quality plywood or

hardwood ⅜″ (10 mm) thick, and cut out with a backsaw. Sand the edges. Drill the two screw axle holes in the bottom edges. Use a drill of smaller diameter than the screws you will use to secure the wheels. These "pilot holes" make putting screws into the wood easier—without a small pilot hole, the plywood might split.

**Wheels.** Cut two wheels from a dowel rod 1″ (25 mm) in diameter. They should be ⅜″ (10 mm) thick. Slice the

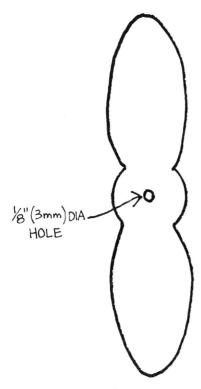

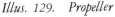

⅛" (3mm) DIA HOLE

*Illus. 129.    Propeller*

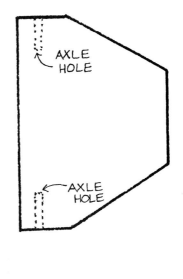

AXLE HOLE

AXLE HOLE

*Illus. 130.    Undercarriage support*

dowel on a bench hook and use a mitre block to aid accurate cutting. Drill a center hole in each wheel using a ⅛" (3 mm) drill bit. Rub the sawn edges smooth with sandpaper.

**Fuselage.** On ¾" (20 mm) thick softwood, mark out the fuselage shape (Illus. 131) and cut out carefully with a backsaw. Smooth the roughness caused by the saw cuts using medium sandpaper wrapped round a flat file. Two slots have to be cut out, one on the top edge for the pilot's cockpit and another underneath into which the undercarriage support is later glued. The latter slot must be cut accurately so that the support fits tightly when glued in place.

To cut out the slots, cut vertically down on the inside of each line to the bottom, using a backsaw. The waste wood has to be cut out using a chisel (Illus. 132).

Next, use a ½" (13 mm) flat-bit drill and drill a hole ½" (13 mm) deep into the pilot cockpit slot.

Now two slots have to be cut at the back of the fuselage to take the tail plane and rudder (Illus. 133). Each slot is 1" (25 mm) deep. Cut out carefully so that the width of the slots match the thickness of the plywood tail plane and rudder. They need to be fairly tight-fitting so that, together with the glue, they are held strongly in place.

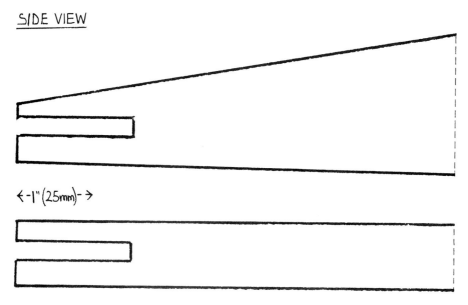

← -1" (25mm) - →

*Illus. 131. Fusilage template, side view (top) and plan view (bottom)*

PLAN VIEW

Mark out the tail plane slot first on both sides of the fuselage. (They should be parallel with the underside of the fuse-lage.) Hold the fuselage in a vise (use scrap wood on either side to protect the wood from being marked by the jaws of the vise), so that you can cut vertically down. It is important to cut with the backsaw blade on the inside of your guidelines, especially since these slots are narrow. Cut out the waste wood using a narrow chisel. (If you have no chisel this small, use a ⅛" [3 mm] drill and pierce the bottom of the slot just above the guideline.)

Then cut the vertical rudder slot. Check that the slots accept the tail and rudder tightly but not too tightly.

**Assembly.** Glue the undercarriage sup-port in its slot. Apply glue to the inside

edges of the tail slots. Slide the tail plane into place, making sure it is balanced. Next, apply a little glue into the rudder slot and slide the rudder into place, glu-ing it onto the tailplane. Leave to dry.

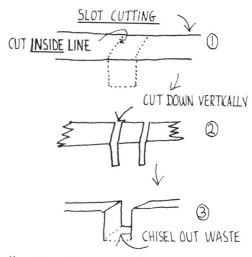

*Illus. 132. How to cut slots*

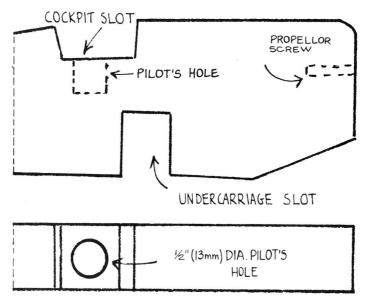

COCKPIT SLOT

PILOT'S HOLE

PROPELLOR SCREW

UNDERCARRIAGE SLOT

½" (13mm) DIA. PILOT'S HOLE

*Illus. 131. (continued)*

Next undercoat the fuselage, tail plane, rudder and undercarriage support. Undercoat the wing, wheels and propeller. Paint the wheels, propeller and wings separately (Color Illus. D2).

Screw the wheels in place, using a cup washer between the screw head and the wheel. Screw on the propeller using a cup washer. Don't tighten the screws; leave enough play so that the wheels and propeller spin freely.

Screw the wing in place (glue it as well for extra strength).

Under the fuselage at the back, just in front of the rudder slot, screw in the little screw eye for the tail wheel.

The finishing touch is to cut a 1″ (25-mm)-long head section off a clothespin, draw on a helmet shape and pilot's face,

seal with varnish and paint the helmet when the varnish is dry. You may have to reduce the diameter of the pin body using sandpaper; so check that the pilot fits in his hole before painting.

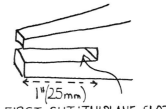

1″ (25mm)

1. FIRST CUT: TAILPLANE SLOT

2. SECOND CUT: RUDDER SLOT

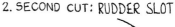

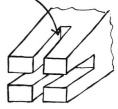

*Illus. 133. Detail of tail plane and rudder slots*

*Illus. 134.*

# Swinging
# Merry-Go-Round

This merry-go-round fascinates children. They set it in motion and it swings back and forth as the tension in the thread winds the platform up and down the dowel rod.

## MATERIALS

Pine, ½″ (13 mm) thick: 4″ (102 mm) × 4″ (102 mm) for each horse; make 3
Plywood, ⅜″ (10 mm) thick: 7½″ (192 mm) × 15″ (381 mm) for two disks
Dowel, ½″ (13 mm) diameter: 12″ (300 mm) long
Small wooden ball
Strong thread

**Horses.** The horses and riders (Illus. 135) are traced out on to the pine and cut out carefully with a coping saw. Make sure that the grain of the wood is vertical, for if not, the horses and riders will not be as strong. Sand smooth the edges, but do not attempt to round off the edges too much. When smooth and clean, draw over your lines with a fine soft-tip or drawing pen, and seal carefully with varnish. (You can separate the riders from the horses using a fretsaw, to add interest, but when I did this, I found that each rider only fitted its own horse, and children will try to force things that they think will fit!)

**Base.** Make from the ⅜″ (10 mm) plywood. Mark out a circle of 3½″ (90 mm) radius and mark the center of the circle clearly, so that you can position the drill bit accurately when you come to drill the hole to hold the dowel rod.

Cut out the disc using a coping saw or a fretsaw with a thick blade, remembering to cut on the waste side (outside of the circle line) of the plywood. Use a ½″ (13 mm) flat bit in an electric drill to drill a hole in the center of the disc. It is essential to get the hole drilled vertically (a pillar drill attachment is very useful!) if

*Illus. 135.  Horse and rider template for Swinging Merry-Go-Round, with alternate faces*

the finished toy is to work easily. Sand the edges of the disc to get a neat circle.

**Dowel Rod.** Cut the dowel rod to length. Before gluing the dowel in place, it is necessary to cut notches in the top of the dowel to hold the threads on which the platform will be suspended. Make three cuts as shown in Illus. 136. Cut the notches for the thread, using a fretsaw, to a depth of about ¼ ″ (6 mm).

After cutting the notches, glue the dowel rod into the hole drilled in the center of the base disc. Wipe off excess glue, and check that the rod is vertical when in place.

**Platform.** To make the platform you now draw another disc the same size as the base. Before cutting out the circle and

drilling out the center hole, it is necessary to mark the positions for the notches and the horses. Illus. 137 shows how to mark out the platform, but note that it is not full size and cannot be traced directly. Use a protractor to divide the 7 ″ (178-mm)-diameter circle into sixths (60°). Three points (A, B and C) are marked to show where the notches (cut with a fretsaw) go on the platform disc. The other points (D, E and F) are rectangles to help locate the horses evenly when you come to glue them in place. The lines are drawn at right angles to the center of the circle (3 ″ [76.4 mm] from the center).

Cut out the disc and drill the center hole. The hole needs to be bigger than ½ ″ (13 mm) in diameter so that the platform moves freely around the dowel. Sand the

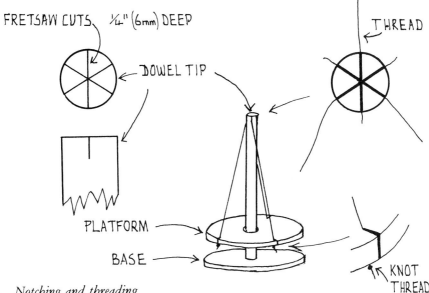

FRETSAW CUTS, ¼″ (6mm) DEEP

DOWEL TIP

THREAD

PLATFORM

BASE

KNOT
THREAD

*Illus. 136.  Notching and threading*

disc edges smooth with sandpaper, and try the platform over the dowel in the base to check that it moves freely. (You can rub the rod with a candle to reduce the friction.)

**Assembling and Threading.** Threading is a bit fiddly! Cut three lengths of strong thread to about 12″ (300 mm). With the platform already located over the dowel peg, knot one end of the thread and pass it into one of the notches on the platform (Illus. 136). Pull gently till the knot touches the underside of the platform. Pass the other end over one of the notches at the top of the dowel and pull gently till the edge of the platform is raised about 1½″ (38 mm) above the base. Repeat with the other two threads, so that the platform is parallel to the base. The notches in the end of the dowel will hold the thread tight.

By now, the platform should be balanced in place, and if turned and spun, should turn up and down the rod freely. Glue the horses in place and decorate when dry. To finish off, I drilled a ½″ (13 mm) hole in a small wooden ball and glued it on top of the dowel rod to conceal the threads and knots (Color Illus. D2).

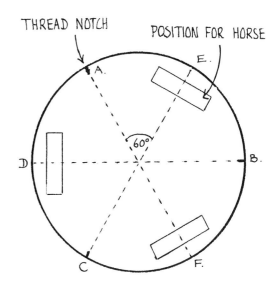

THREAD NOTCH

POSITION FOR HORSE

E.

60°

D

B.

C

F.

*Illus. 137.  Guide for marking out the platform (not full size)*

*Illus. 138.*

# Merry-Go-Round

This merry-go-round with its clothespin passengers simply spins on a rounded dowel rod. My youngest child loves removing and replacing the clothespin people! To add interest to the toy, I attached an old bell to the base and suspended washers on the underside of the platform; so that, as the merry-go-round spins, the washers gently ring the bell.

## MATERIALS

### Base

Blockboard or softwood, ¾″ (20 mm) thick: 7½″ (190 mm) × 7½″ (190 mm)
Dowel, ½″ (13 mm) diameter: 7″ (178 mm) long

### Platform

Plywood, ⅜″ (10 mm) thick: 7½″ (190 mm) × 7½″ (190 mm)
12 wooden clothespins

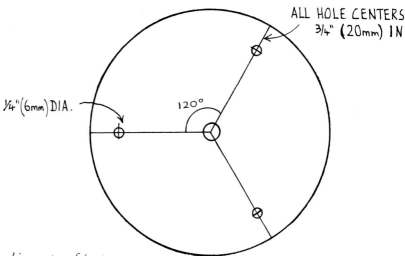

ALL HOLE CENTERS
3/4" (20mm) IN

1/4"(6mm) DIA.

120°

*Illus. 139.   Guide for marking out roof (not full size)*

## Roof

Blockboard or softwood, ¾ " (20 mm) thick: 7½ " (190 mm) × 7½ " (190 mm) Dowel, ¼ " (6 mm) diameter: 18 " (460 mm) long

**Base.** To make the base, mark out a 7 " (178-mm)-diameter circle on the blockboard with pencil and compass. Make sure that the center of the circle is clearly marked with the compass point, so that you can accurately position the drill when cutting out the hole to hold the dowel rod.

Cut out the disc using a coping saw and sand. Drill a ½ " (13-mm)-diameter hole in the center of the disc all the way through the wood. (Remember to put a piece of waste wood underneath.) Cut the ½ " (13-mm)-diameter dowel rod to a length of 7 " (178 mm). It is necessary to point or round off the top end of the dowel carefully, so that the platform spins freely. Using coarse-grade sandpaper

wrapped around a flat file, round off the top of the dowel, leaving the centermost point at its original height. Smooth with fine sandpaper and steel wool to reduce the friction when the merry-go-round spins. (You can rub the smooth point of the dowel with candle wax to further reduce the friction.)

Glue the dowel rod into the base and wipe off excess glue with a damp cloth. Make sure that the dowel is vertical in its place.

**Roof.** Draw out a 7 " (178-mm)-diameter circle using pencil and compass and cut out and smooth edges, as for the base. Mark the center of the circle clearly. Three holes have to be drilled to take the ¼ " (6-mm)-diameter dowels which support the roof. A protractor is used to mark the position of the holes. Divide the circle into three parts, 120° each, and draw light guidelines from the center of the circle to the circumference. Each hole

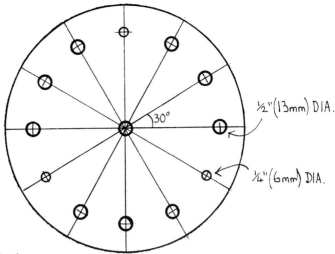

½" (13mm) DIA.

¼" (6mm) DIA.

30°

*Illus. 140.  Guide for marking out platform* (*not full size*)

center is ¾ " (20 mm) from the circumference. (Illus. 138 shows the relationships but is not full scale.)

Drill out three ¼ " (6 mm) holes to a depth of ½ " (13 mm). Make sure they are vertical and that you don't go right through the roof! Drill out the ½ " (13 mm) center hole to a depth of ½ " (13 mm). Clean off any roughness caused by drilling with sandpaper.

**Platform.** Mark out a 7 " (178-mm)-diameter circle out of ⅜ " (10-mm)-thick plywood and use a fretsaw to cut out the disc. Use sandpaper, as before, on the roof and base to prepare the edges. Next, you must mark the positions of the three roof support holes and the nine holes for the clothespin passengers, which are shown small-scale in Illus. 140. Use a protractor and divide the platform disc into 12, by marking off 30° angles as shown in the diagram. Draw in light guidelines to the edge of the disc. Each hole center should

be ¾ " (20 mm) in from the edge. Mark the centers with the point of a compass.

Careful marking out and drilling is essential. The drill must be kept vertical. You should clamp the disc to a piece of waste wood to avoid the plywood splitting. All the holes on the platform go right through the plywood.

Drill the three roof support holes (using a ¼ " [6 mm] drill), then the ½ " (13 mm) holes for the pegs, drilling the center hole in the disc with the same drill.

At this point you should cut the three rods which support the roof from ¼ " (6-mm)-diameter dowel so that each is 5½ " (140 mm) in length.

**Assembly.** The center hole in the platform should spin freely around the rod in the base (Illus. 141). Try it and slightly enlarge the center hole if it doesn't move freely, using a pencil wrapped with medium-grade sandpaper.

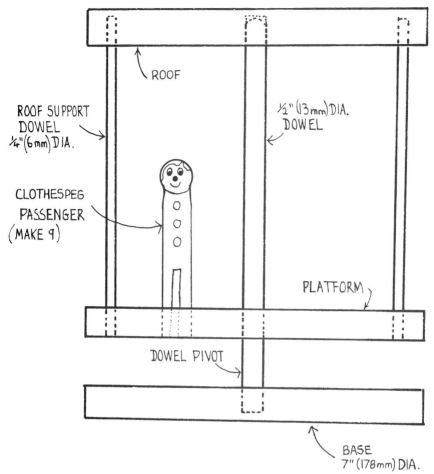

ROOF

ROOF SUPPORT
DOWEL
¼" (6mm) DIA.

½" (13mm) DIA.
DOWEL

CLOTHESPEG
PASSENGER
(MAKE 9)

PLATFORM

DOWEL PIVOT

BASE
7" (178mm) DIA.

*Illus. 141.   Diagram of Merry-Go-Round, side view*

Glue the roof-supporting dowels into the underside of the roof and in place on the platform. Check that the two discs are parallel. Wipe off excess glue.

When dry, place the assembled roof and platform over the dowel pivot. It should spin nicely. If not, adjust the point at the end of the pivot by sanding if necessary.

The clothespin passengers are cut to a length of 2½″ (65 mm). Use medium

and fine sandpaper to get the surfaces of the clothespins smooth and then rub with steel wool. When the pegs are all cleaned and smoothed, use a fine soft-tip pen to draw on the faces. Then varnish carefully to avoid smearing the lines, and also seal the rest of the peg. When dry, paint with enamel paints (Color Illus. D2). A second coat may be needed to get a really nice finish.

*Illus. 142.*

# Peg Box Game

Each player has a set of different-colored pegs. They take it in turns to spin the arrow. If the arrow points to a color in their possession, they post it in the appropriate hole. The first to post all their pegs is the winner. Pegs are stored in the box between times.

As well as helping young children to recognize colors, this game helps children to overcome their youthful aversion to taking turns!

## MATERIALS
### Box
Plywood, ¼″ (6 mm) thick: 8″ (203 mm) × 8″ (203 mm) for the lid

Plywood, ½″ (13 mm) thick: 3½″ (90 mm) × 16″ (406 mm) for two 8″ (203 mm) long sides

Plywood, ½″ (13 mm) thick: 3½″ (90 mm) × 14″ (356 mm) for two 7″ (178 mm) long sides

Plywood or hardboard, ¼″ (6 mm) thick: 8″ (203 mm) × 8″ (203 mm) for the base

### Arrow
Plywood, ⅛″ (3 mm) thick: ¾″ (20 mm) × 7½″ (190 mm)

### Pegs
Dowel, ¾″ (20 mm) diameter: 24″ (610 mm) long to make 12 pegs

**Miscellaneous**
Small nut and bolt: 1″ (25 mm) long
Washers
Enamel paints or wood stains: six different colors
Varnish

**Box.** The sides of the box are cut from ½″ (13-mm)-thick plywood; make 2 sides 8″ (203 mm) × 3½″ (89 mm) and 2 sides 7″ (178 mm) × 3½″ (89 mm).

Or, you can buy softwood which will do the job as well, and has the added advantage that you can get your lumber dealer to cut it accurately to the required width; all you have to do then is cut it to the right lengths.

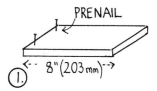

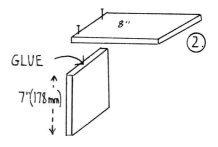

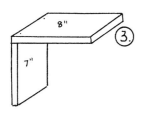

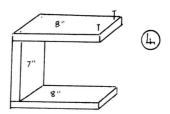

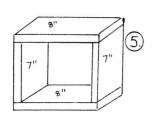

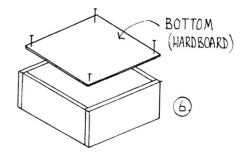

*Illus. 143.   Making the peg box*

As shown in Illus. 143, take one 8″ (203 mm) × 3½″ (89 mm) side and on a flat surface, tap 1″ (25 mm) finishing nails shallowly into the corners of one end, making sure that the nails go in straight and that they are ¼″ (6 mm) from the edge.

Next, take a 7″ (178 mm) piece and smear one short edge with glue. Place the prenailed piece in position and tap the nails down, making sure that the pieces don't slide out of position. (The finishing nails, by the way, only hold the wood in position while the adhesive dries.)

Turn the two pieces you have fixed together upside down. Glue and nail the other 8″ (203 mm) piece in place, taking care to line it up properly.

Finally, smear the short-end edges of the remaining 7″ (178 mm) piece with glue,

slide carefully in place and tap in the finishing nails.

**Base.** The base is made from ¼″ (6 mm) plywood or hardboard and can either be cut to size 8″ (203 mm) × 8″ (203 mm) or, if you wish, you can place the box frame over an off-cut of plywood or hardboard and trace around the frame (especially when your box isn't quite square!).

Glue the underside edges of the box frame, tap in ½″ (13 mm) finishing nails or brads; one for each corner should be plenty.

**Lid.** The lid is made from ¼″ (6 mm) plywood, 8″ (203 mm) × 8″ (203 mm). Marking out according to Illus. 144 looks complicated but it is quite straightforward. The lid has six evenly spaced holes through which the children post dowel pegs, and is also divided off into sections.

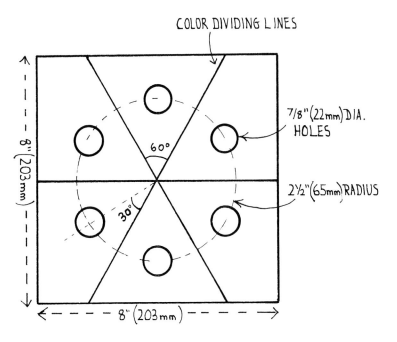

*Illus. 144. Marking out the peg box lid*

Each section has a separate color to correspond with the colors of the pegs.

First, find the center of the 8″ (203-mm)-square piece you have cut out by drawing diagonal lines from each corner. Where the lines cross, place the point of the compass and draw a pencilled circle of 2½″ (65 mm) radius. This gives the distance from the center of the holes for posting the dowels.

Next, draw on the guidelines for coloring the sections. Use a protractor to divide off 60° sections as shown in the diagram. The centers for the ⅞″ (22 mm) holes to be drilled are found by marking off 30° sections which space the holes evenly between the color guidelines. The position for each of the holes is where the 30° lines cross the circle you drew. Mark them clearly with a compass point. Drill each hole carefully.

A ⅛″ (3 mm) hole is also drilled in the center of the square lid, through which, later, a small nut and bolt will be used to secure the spinning arrow. Check that the lid sits evenly on the box frame. To hold it in place and also allow it to be easily removed, cut out pieces of softwood ½″ (13 mm) square and glue to the underside of the lid just over ½″ (13 mm) in from each edge.

**Decoration.** To decorate the box, use the guidelines already drawn on the lid, and extend them down the box sides. If you paint the box, remember to seal it first with varnish or an appropriate undercoat. I used six different wood stains. I scored

the guidelines with a utility knife, so that as I applied each stain, one color didn't spread over another. (Obviously, coloring the dowel pegs was made easier and quicker by using stains also.)

**Arrow.** The pointer arrow is cut from ⅛″ (3 mm) plywood that is 7½″ (190 mm) long and ¾″ (20 mm) wide (Illus. 145). A ⅛″ (3 mm) diameter hole is cut in the position shown on the diagram at the midpoint, so that it can be fixed to the lid with the aid of a small nut and bolt. You will need to pack small washers between the lid and the pointer to stop the arrow dragging as it spins.

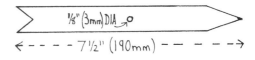

*Illus. 145.  Pointer diagram (not full size)*

**Pegs.** Finally, you need to cut 12 dowel pegs out of ¾″ (20-mm)-diameter dowel to a length of 2″ (50 mm) each. This gives you enough for two pegs for each color section. The box will of course easily accommodate more if more playing pieces are wanted. Use a bench hook to cut the pegs to length, and use the addition of a mitre block as well if you find it hard to cut straight. Take care as you cut the dowel, especially when you are nearly through, as it often splits if you aren't careful. Sand off any roughness, seal and then color.

*Illus. 146.*

# Two Climbing Toys

Both the British fireman and sailor climbing toys work on the same principle and are very straightforward to make. They are suspended from hangers on a loop of string which passes through holes drilled through the hands. The child pulls both strings taut and then applies downward pressure on each string in turn. The toy climbs the string and slides down again when the pressure is released. Although very young children are fascinated by the toy, I would not recommend it for under-fives to use unsupervised!

## MATERIALS

Softwood, ¾″ (20 mm) thick: 6″ (150 mm) × 8″ (200 mm)
Softwood, 1″ (25 mm) thick: 1″ (25 mm) × 6″ (150 mm)
Thin nylon cord or strong string: 120″ (3 mm)
1 cup hook for hanging cups
2 small wooden beads

Trace and copy one of the outlines (Illus. 148 or 149) onto a clean, smooth piece of softwood ¾″ (20 mm) thick, 6″ (150 mm) × 8″ (200 mm). Cut out the outline shape with a coping saw on the waste side of the outline.

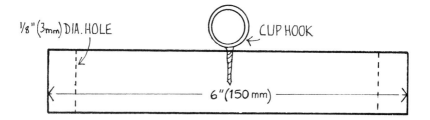

*Illus. 147.  Hanger diagram*

Next, spend a little time sanding the sawn edges with coarse and then medium grade sandpaper. You need smooth regular edges and, since the toy is to be painted, it is worth remembering that paint won't conceal any roughness you leave on the edges; so rub away the saw "scars." Round over any sharp edges.

Then, drill the two holes in the hands indicated on the template by dashed lines. Use a ⅛″ (3 mm) drill bit. It is easiest to drill the holes with the toy held upside down in a vise. Drill centrally at the angle indicated, and sand off any roughness caused by drilling.

Next, cut a 6″ (150 mm) length of softwood 1″ (25 mm) × 1″ (25 mm) to make the hanger (Illus. 147). Two holes are drilled in the hanger 5″ (127 mm) apart. Screw the cup hook centrally into the hanger bar.

Before threading, the next step is to paint the toy. I sealed my toy with varnish, having given it a final rub with fine-grade sandpaper and steel wool, and traced on the main features to act as guidelines for painting. If you use an undercoat, of course you will have to draw on your fea-

ture lines after it has dried. The colors I used are blue, white, black and natural wood for skin tone. I applied a second coat of each enamel color to get a really nice finish.

Cut two lengths of string or cord 48″ (1220 mm). Thread a wooden bead on each and knot the end of the string. Pass the unknotted end through the hole in one arm so that the bead rests under the arm. The unknotted end is then passed through one of the holes in the hanger and knotted above. Make sure that the knot is large and sturdy enough so that when in use, the downward pressure doesn't pull it out. Thread the other side in the same way. Next cut a 12″ (300 mm) length of string and tie it to the cup hook to form a loop to hang the toy from the ceiling.

⅛"(3mm) DIA.
HOLE

*Illus. 148. British Sailor
Climbing Toy*

FIRE

⅛″ (3mm) DIA. HOLE

*Illus. 149. British Fireman Climbing Toy*

*Illus. 150.*

# Cat Fishing Game

This toy is double-sided so that two children can play. All the fish are removed from their hooks on the cat body and placed on the floor around the cat. With a fishing pole each, the children sit on each side of the cat and pick up the fish with the little magnets at the end of their line, then try to hang the fish on the hooks on their side of the cat. The first player with all their fish in place is the winner.

## MATERIALS

Plywood, ⅜″ (9 mm) thick: 7″ (180 mm) × 11″ (280 mm) for the cat body

Softwood, 1½″ (40 mm) thick: 5″ (128 mm) × 5″ (128 mm) for the base

Dowel, ¼″ (6 mm) diameter: 20″ (510 mm) length for the fishing poles

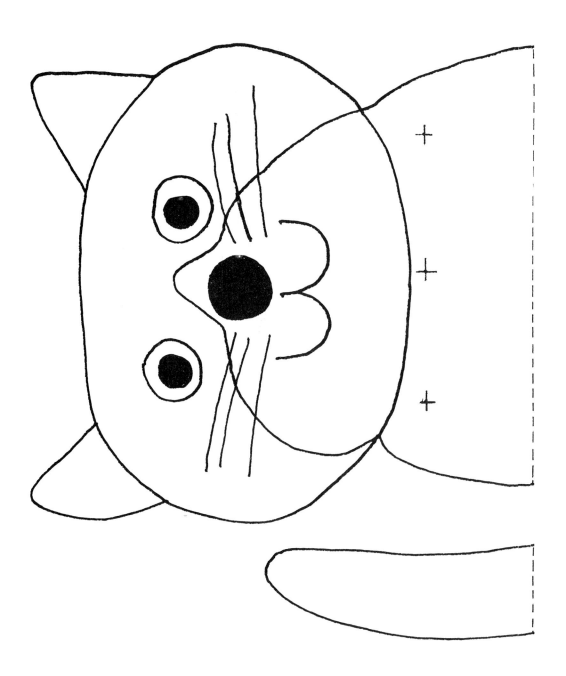

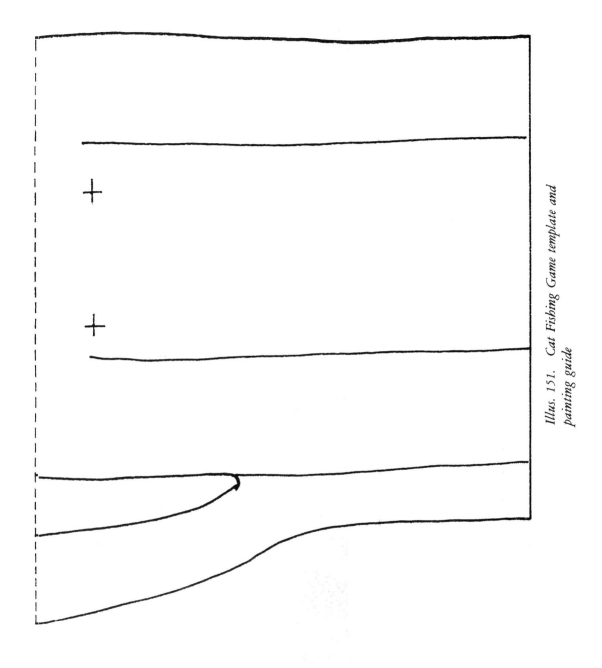

*Illus. 151. Cat Fishing Game template and painting guide*

Softwood or plywood, ¼″ (6 mm) thick: off-cuts for the fish
10 small screw eyes and 10 screw hooks in matching sizes
2 small magnets
Strong thread: 24″ (610 mm) long

Mark out the cat outline (Illus. 151) on the plywood and cut it out using a thick fretsaw blade. Sand and smooth the edges with medium and then fine sandpaper. Clean up the flat surfaces of the plywood with fine sandpaper in the direction of the grain. Trace on all the feature lines on both sides of the cat shape. The decoration used later is wood stain; so do not seal at this stage.

To make the circular base, draw a circle of 5″ (128 mm) diameter on the softwood. In order to get a circle, it is necessary to take off as much waste wood as possible using a backsaw to slice off tangents on the waste side of the wood. Use a flat file on the edges to reduce roughness and sand the edges with coarse and then medium-grade sandpaper to achieve a smooth circular block. Cut across the diameter of the block with the backsaw, so that you have two semicircular blocks. These are glued in place to each side of the cat body to form a base.

Next, mark out the shapes of ten little fish on the ¼″ (6-mm)-thick softwood from Illus. 152. Cut out the shapes with a fretsaw, and smooth and round the edges with medium and then fine sandpaper. Draw the feature lines on each fish using a fine black drawing pen. Seal each fish with varnish.

Screw one small screw eye into the nose edge of each little fish. Cut the dowel rod to two 10″ (255 mm) lengths, tie magnets with thread and attach threads to magnets and tie opposite ends to fishing poles. Two holes can then be drilled into the base to hold the fishing poles when they are not in use.

Both sides of the cat should be decorated in the same way. The whole of the cat body is stained with a light brown wood stain, but the face remains natural. To achieve this, mark the boundaries of the face with a sharp blade and then carefully seal the face area with varnish. Then stain the rest of the cat body with a light brown stain. The fur markings are simply painted on using a darker brown stain. Don't overload the brush or the stain will spread too far (try on waste plywood first).

Seal the whole surface and use black enamel to highlight facial feature lines. Gloss white enamel around the eye completes the painting (Color Illus. D2).

When both sides are dry, screw the hooks in position on the cat.

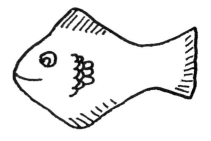

*Illus. 152.  Fish template and painting guide*

# Jointed Monkey

I was fascinated when I was a child by toys which moved when you pulled a string, and this monkey fulfilled my ambition to make such a toy.

## MATERIALS

Plywood, ⅛″ (3 mm) thick: 6″ (153 mm) × 9″ (230 mm)
8 small aluminum rivets: ⅛″ (3 mm) in diameter
8 small washers: ⅛″ (3 mm)
String
Strong thread
Thin cardboard for spacers

Draw the component parts on to the plywood and cut out the five pieces (Illus. 155), using a fine fretsaw blade. Mark the positions of the ten drill centers, and carefully drill out the holes using a drill bit of slightly larger diameter than ⅛″ (3 mm), so that the joints move freely when assembled. Pierce the plywood above hip and shoulder rivet holes to take the strong thread, as indicated on the drawing.

The face and ears are left the natural color of the plywood; so you need to score the outlines of these areas using a blade. Then carefully varnish the areas, so that the dark stain used for the rest of the toy won't penetrate the areas you want to remain the natural color. Rub or brush all the components, back, front and edges, with dark brown stain, having rubbed all the edges smooth with fine sandpaper. Seal the toy with varnish and allow to dry.

*Illus. 153.*

Jointing is achieved using rivets. These soft metal fixings are normally used for joining thin sheets of metal tightly together, but to permit the animal's limbs to move freely, the rivets must be fitted loosely. To do this, you have to insert thin spacers of cardboard between the surfaces to be riveted, which can be removed after the rivet has been "set." So the rivet

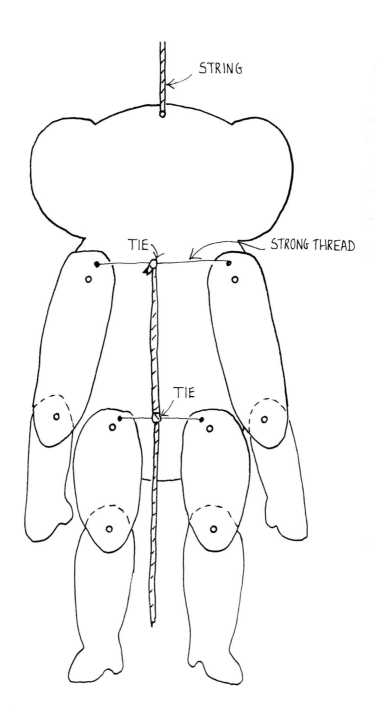

STRING

STRONG THREAD

TIE

TIE

*Illus. 154. Diagram of holes for string and rivets*

150 ▪ JOINTED MONKEY

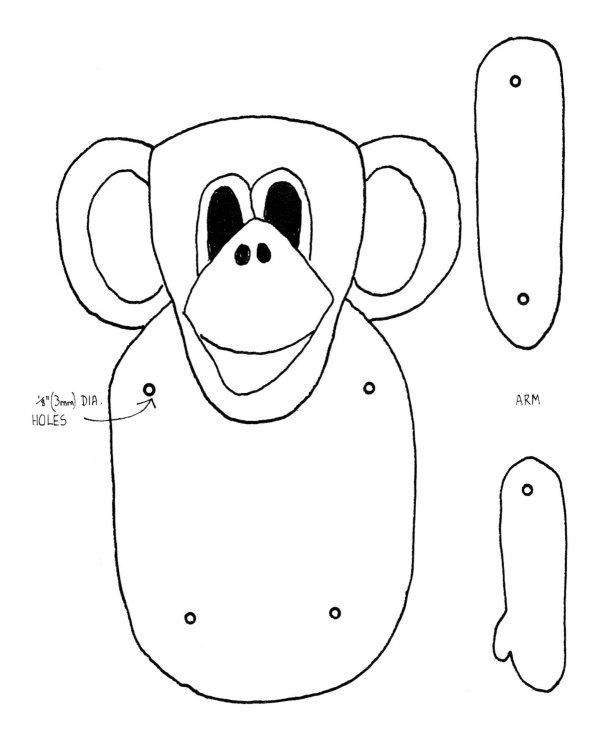

1/8"(3mm) DIA. HOLES

ARM

*Illus. 155.   Jointed Monkey templates*
(*continued on page 152*)

has to be long enough to accommodate two thicknesses of the plywood plus the washers.

There are several kinds of rivet on the market. I used pop rivets, which are squeezed tight using a special (but inexpensive) rivet gun, but I had to splay the ends on the underside of the toy over a small washer by gently tapping out the center with a Phillips (cross-headed) screwdriver. Alternatively, you may use a rivet set, which flattens the soft rivet head.

Strong thread is threaded through the tiny holes indicated in Illus. 154, above the rivet holes connecting shoulder to shoulder and hip to hip. Thread these loosely before riveting, if necessary, and tighten before knotting. A pull string is tied on to each connecting thread, as shown in Illus. 154, so that when the string is pulled down, the limbs move simultaneously. A string is also attached to the head for hanging the toy.

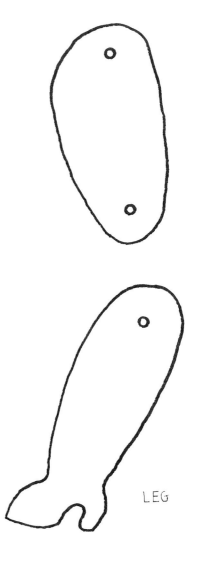

*Illus. 155. Jointed Monkey templates (continued from page 151)*

# Hickory Dickory Clock

This toy, in the shape of a grandfather clock, combines a "teaching clock," a dowel-rod run down which a little mouse rattles, and a base on which days of the week can be indicated by a removable peg placed against the appropriate day of the week (Illus. 156). The toy is made in three parts. At the top is a clock base, the day board base is at the bottom, and the long narrow rattle board forms the middle. The clock base and day board are screwed on to the ends of the rattle board.

## MATERIALS

### Clock Base
Plywood, ½″ (13 mm) thick: 7″ (180 mm) × 8″ (215 mm)
Plywood, ⅛″ (3 mm) thick: 6½″ (165 mm) × 6½″ (165 mm) for the clock dial
Plywood, ⅛″ (3 mm) thick: scraps to make clock hands
Nut and bolt: ⅛″ (3 mm) diameter
Small washers
Rub-on numbers

### Rattle Board
Plywood, ½″ (13 mm) thick: 4½″ (115 mm) × 36½″ (925 mm)
Dowel, ¼″ (6 mm) diameter: 24″ (610 mm) long

### Day Board Base
Plywood, ½″ (13 mm) thick: 6½″ (165 mm) × 8½″ (215 mm)
Rub-on lettering

**Mouse.** To start, mark out the mouse outline (Illus. 157) by tracing or using carbon paper on to an off-cut of ¼″ (6

*Illus. 156.*

*Illus. 157. Mouse template and painting guide*

mm) plywood. Cut out the outline shape using a fretsaw with a medium thickness blade. Draw on the feature lines which later act as guidelines when you paint it. The distance between the curves where the bottom of the mouse's ears meet the head is important, and the curve may have to be adjusted when the rattle board is assembled if the mouse doesn't run down the clock easily (Illus. 163).

**Day Baseboard.** Next, tackle the day board base. Cut out an 8½" (215 mm) × 6½" (165 mm) rectangle of ½" (13 mm) plywood. A guideline is drawn along the left 8½" (215 mm) side 1" (25 mm) from the edge, and the positions of the holes to be drilled are marked off at even intervals along the guideline (Illus. 158). The interval between each of the

seven hole centers is 1¼" (30 mm). Drill out the holes with a ¼" (6 mm) drill. Cut a short 1½" (40 mm) length of ¼" (6 mm) dowel, which is used to indicate the day of the week. The days of the week are "written" on the base using bold rub-on lettering, placed in line with the appropriate hole.

**Clock Baseboard.** The half-scale diagram of the clock baseboard (Illus. 159) shows the decorative top edge common to many real grandfather clocks. To make the clock baseboard, first cut out the rectangle from ½" (13 mm) plywood to size 8½" (215 mm) × 7" (180 mm).

Next, mark each of the 7" (180 mm) edges halfway along, and draw a lightly pencilled line to give you a midpoint for aligning the clock dial center and to help

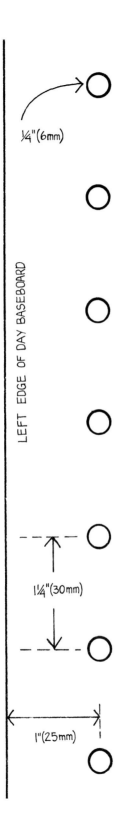

position the small circular cutout at the top edge of the clock base. Next, draw a circle 1″ (25 mm) in diameter placing the point of the compass ½″ (13 mm) in from the edge on the middle line you have drawn.

Use a T-square and draw a light line 1″ (25 mm) in from the top edge to give you the sloping lines shown in the diagram. Cut out the circle with a fretsaw or 1″ (25-mm)-diameter flat bit drill. Cut the sloping edges off with a backsaw and sand off any rough edges with sandpaper.

Next, using a fine-toothed fretsaw blade, cut out a circle of ⅛″ (3-mm)-thick plywood of 6″ (153 mm) diameter, marking the center of the circle clearly. Use a protractor to divide up the circle into 30° segments and draw in light guidelines, which will later help you place the clock dial rub-on numbers. Drill out the ⅛″ (3 mm) center hole.

The disc that forms the clock dial is glued in place. To find the position where the center hole in the clock dial sits and to align the clock dial before gluing, measure along the middle line drawn earlier 3½″ (90 mm) from the bottom edge. Drill the ½″ (13 mm) plywood base at this point with a ⅛″ (3 mm) drill (which you also use later when you align the dial to the base).

Trace the designs of the clock hands (Illus. 160) onto ⅛″ (3 mm) plywood, cut out with a fretsaw and drill the two holes out.

*Illus. 158. Peg holes for day baseboard*

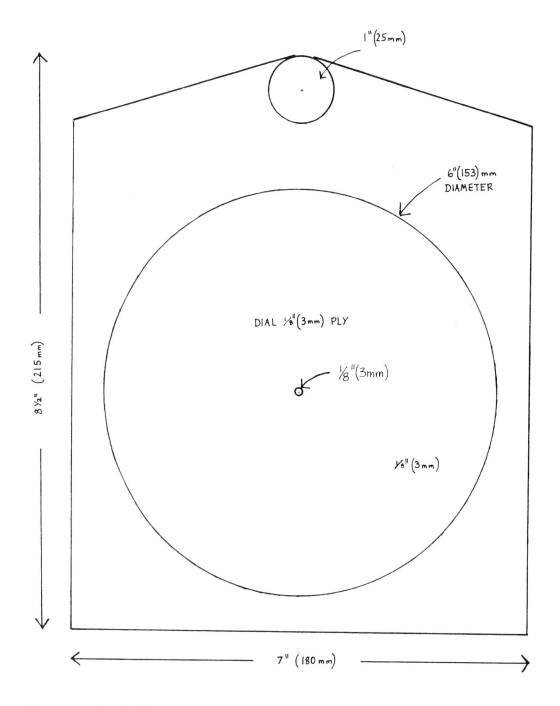

1"(25mm)

6"(153)mm
DIAMETER

8½" (215mm)

DIAL ⅛"(3mm) PLY

⅛"(3mm)

⅛"(3mm)

7" (180mm)

*Illus. 159. Clock baseboard, drawn to half
scale*

**Rattle Board.** Both the clock baseboard and the day baseboard are screwed in place over the narrow rattle board. So at each end of the board, 3″ (76 mm) of the rattle board is concealed when the clock is assembled. Illus. 161 shows the spacing of the first six peg holes full scale, working from the bottom upwards. Illus. 162 shows how this segment relates to the entire dimensions of the board. Cut out the oblong 36½″ (925 mm) × 4½″ (165 mm) (your lumber dealer could save you a lot of sawing by cutting the plywood to width for you!) and mark a line across the width using a T-square to mark off the first four inches. The bottom of Illus. 161 is the line you have just drawn!

**Marking the Rattle Board.** The success of the toy depends on accurate spacing of the dowel pegs on the rattle board; so great care should be taken when marking out and drilling.

To begin, you must draw two guidelines the whole length of the board 1″ (25 mm) in and parallel to the edge. Hole centers A and B are horizontally in line 5″ (127 mm) from the bottom edge of the board. They are rests to hold the mouse in place on the board at the end of his run. The distance from A to D is

2¾″ (70 mm). Mark the position of D and proceed along the left-hand side guideline marking off at 2¾″ (70 mm) intervals. You should have ten drill centers on the left-hand guideline.

On the right-hand side guideline, the drill centers are staggered. So, drill center point C is 1⅜″ (35 mm) from point B. Now from drill center C proceed to mark off along the guideline again at 2¾″ (70 mm) intervals. (You may find a set of dividers useful for marking off the intervals.)

You should have 11 drill centers marked in altogether on the right-hand side guideline.

**Drilling the Rattle Board.** Use a ¼″ (6 mm) drill bit and drill out each of the 21 holes in which you will later glue the dowel pegs. Take care to position the tip of the drill bit exactly over the drill center marked on the plywood, and try to drill vertically. I drilled my holes all the way through the thickness of the plywood.

Use a backsaw to cut out 21 dowel pegs, each to a length of 1¼″ (30 mm). Sand the rough ends smooth with medium sandpaper and glue them in their holes. Wipe off excess glue with a damp cloth.

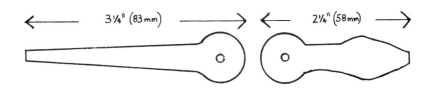

*Illus. 160.   Clock hands*

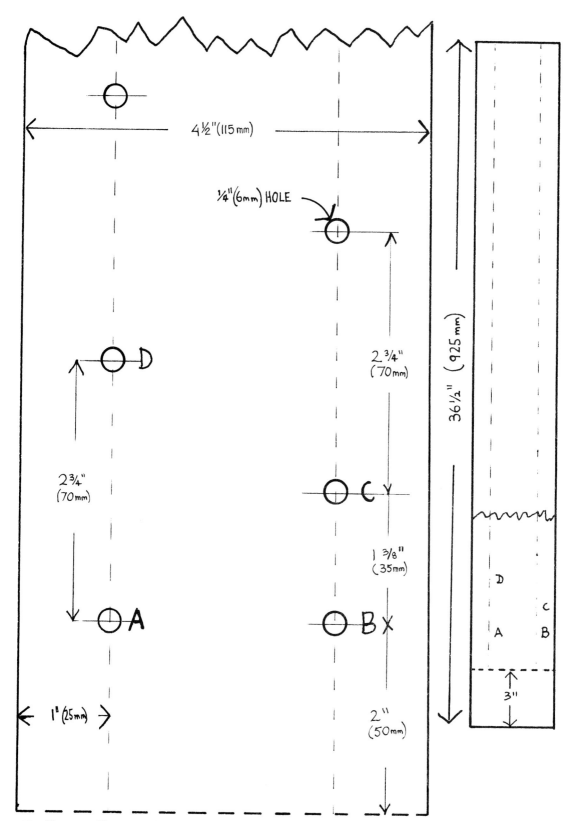

4½"(115mm)

¼"(6mm) HOLE

2¾" (70mm)

D

2¾" (70mm)

C

1 ⅜" (35mm)

A

B

1" (25mm)

2" (50mm)

36½" (925mm)

D

C

A

B

3"

*Illus. 161 (opposite, left). Diagram of bottom peg holes in rattle board, drawn to scale*

*Illus. 162 (opposite, right). Rattle board diagram*

AREA OF
ADJUSTMENT

*Illus. 163.*

**Final Assembly and Finishing.** Before assembling the parts of the toy, lean the rattle board against a wall so that it is almost vertical and place the mouse shape at the top of the run of dowels. Let him go and with luck he should proceed on his ears all the way down the run of dowel pegs. If your mouse sticks halfway down (and you have lined the dowels up carefully), then you need to narrow the distance between the curves under his ears a little, using sandpaper wrapped around a pencil (Illus 163).

The clock baseboard is screwed to the top of the rattle board from behind, allowing a 3″ (76 mm) overlap. The day baseboard is screwed to the bottom of the rattle board from behind allowing a 3″ (76 mm) overlap (Illus. 164). To add an authentic look, add three lengths of moulding glued and nailed in the three places shown in Illus. 164.

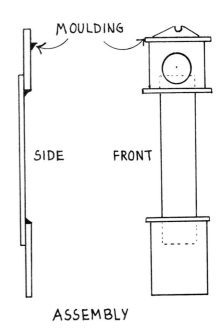

MOULDING

SIDE     FRONT

ASSEMBLY

*Illus. 164. Clock assembly diagram*

# INDEX